T0316600

Cambridge Elements ≡

Elements in Politics and Society in East Asia
edited by
Erin Aeran Chung
Johns Hopkins University
Mary Alice Haddad
Wesleyan University
Benjamin L. Read
University of California, Santa Cruz

STATE, SOCIETY, AND MARKETS IN NORTH KOREA

Andrew Yeo
The Catholic University of America

CAMBRIDGE
UNIVERSITY PRESS

CAMBRIDGE
UNIVERSITY PRESS

University Printing House, Cambridge CB2 8BS, United Kingdom

One Liberty Plaza, 20th Floor, New York, NY 10006, USA

477 Williamstown Road, Port Melbourne, VIC 3207, Australia

314–321, 3rd Floor, Plot 3, Splendor Forum, Jasola District Centre,
New Delhi – 110025, India

103 Penang Road, #05–06/07, Visioncrest Commercial, Singapore 238467

Cambridge University Press is part of the University of Cambridge.

It furthers the University's mission by disseminating knowledge in the pursuit of
education, learning, and research at the highest international levels of excellence.

www.cambridge.org
Information on this title: www.cambridge.org/9781108744799
DOI: 10.1017/9781108888592

First published 2021

A catalogue record for this publication is available from the British Library.

ISBN 978-1-108-74479-9 Paperback
ISSN 2632-7368 (online)
ISSN 2632-735X (print)

State, Society, and Markets in North Korea

Elements in Politics and Society in East Asia

DOI: 10.1017/9781108888592
First published online: September 2021

Andrew Yeo
The Catholic University of America
Author for correspondence: Andrew Yeo, yeo@cua.edu

Abstract: Under Kim Jong-un, North Korea has experienced growing economic markets, an emerging 'nouveau riche,' and modest levels of urban development. To what extent is North Korean politics and society changing? How has the growth of markets transformed state-society relations? This Element evaluates the shifting relationship between state, society, and markets in a deeply authoritarian context. If the regime implements controlled economic measures, extracts rent, and subsumes the market economy into its ideology, the state will likely retain strong authoritarian control. Conversely, if it fails to incorporate markets into its legitimating message, as private actors build informal trust networks, share information, and collude with state bureaucrats, more fundamental changes in state-society relations are in store. By opening the 'black box' of North Korea, this Element reveals how the country manages to teeter forward, and where its domestic future may lie.

Keywords: North Korea, political economy, authoritarian rule, civil society, marketization

ISBNs: 9781108744799 (PB), 9781108888592 (OC)
ISSNs: 2632-7368 (online), 2632-735X (print)

Contents

1 Introduction: State, Society, and Markets in North Korea

To what extent is change taking place in North Korean politics and society? How has the growth of a market economy shifted state-society relations? Given the repressive, totalitarian nature of the North Korean state, the prospect for domestic change appears dim. Yet over the past two decades, the rise of formal and informal markets in North Korea has resulted in limited economic and social change. This includes the emergence of a new moneyed class (the *donju*) and a middle-class lifestyle for a growing number of urban dwellers in Pyongyang and a few other cities along the Sino-North Korea border and coastal ports.

The rise of markets in North Korea is undeniable. However, the extent to which markets are fostering change in state-society relations is debatable. Drawing on evidence from existing surveys and interviews with North Korean defectors and experts, this Element investigates the shifting relationship between markets, state, and society in North Korea. One school of thought remains more optimistic about change as markets begin to hollow out the state-controlled economy. The rise of markets facilitates the exchange of information, giving rise to new informal trust networks that partially operate outside the purview of government control. As North Koreans become increasingly dependent on markets rather than the state for survival, the regime's legitimacy and authority will decline – creating potential space for an emerging public sphere.

The second, and prevailing perspective among North Korea experts is that markets remain embedded within the state, and hence under the watchful eye of the regime. Government officials and state institutions are willing participants in markets. Markets supply state coffers with much-needed revenue, thereby keeping the regime afloat. The growth of markets therefore sustains if not strengthens the regime.

This Element evaluates these two contending views about the relationship between markets, state, and society in North Korea. If the growth of markets creates a gap between state and society and greater space for informal trust networks, horizontal information flow, and increasing opportunities for every-day resistance, we may begin to see greater prospects for societal change. However, if markets empower the state relative to society, we should expect much more limited change in North Korean politics and society. This is especially true if the regime manages to successfully co-opt market actors and take credit for expanding markets, ultimately keeping its legitimacy intact.

To make sense of North Korea today and where it is heading, I apply insights from the literature in political science on autocratic rule, civil society, and state-society relations. I also draw on evidence from existing surveys with North Korean defectors, interviews with North Korea-based field-workers (i.e. foreigners who have lived or worked in North Korea), and information from official North Korean publications. In this opening section, I provide an analytical framework for understanding state-society relations in an authoritarian context. Section 2 focuses on the North Korean state and the regime's autocratic rule. Section 3 explores the rise of markets in North Korea and the symbiotic relationship between state and markets. Section 4 draws on defector surveys and expert interviews to address how markets have shifted state-society relations, taking a closer look at informal trust networks and a nascent public sphere. Section 5 concludes by addressing how external actors such as the United States, China, and South Korea, and exogenous factors such as the COVID-19 pandemic, have shaped domestic trends in North Korea.

1.1 The State and Authoritarian Control

Any analysis of state-society relations in North Korea must begin with the state given its totalitarian nature. As reported by the United Nations Commission of Inquiry on Human Rights in the Democratic People's Republic of Korea (DPRK), the North Korean regime "seeks to dominate every aspect of its citizens' lives and terrorize them from within" (UNCOI 2014, 15). The state restricts freedom of thought, movement, expression, and religion. In addition to severe political repression, the regime controls access to information and keeps its citizens isolated from the outside world. Arbitrary detention, torture, executions, forced disappearances, and prison labor camps remain central to the state's coercive apparatus (Fahy 2019). The regime's multilayer surveillance system penetrates into the daily lives of North Koreans, including attendance at weekly ideological indoctrination and self-criticism sessions that is required of all citizens. Official discourse, symbols, and propaganda flood the public sphere as citizens become "habituated to the cult" of the regime and comply with its rules (Wedeen 2015, 147).

The North Korean regime is often cast as unique – a state that remains unparalleled in the contemporary world given the "gravity, scale and nature" of rights violations (UNCOI 2014, 15). North Korea may very well stand in a league of its own given its degree of isolation from the rest of the world. Yet, the country also follows familiar patterns of authoritarian rule found in other autocratic regimes, and especially in personalist dictatorships. The literature on comparative authoritarian rule can thus shed light on our understanding of the North Korean state.

Autocratic rulers rely on a combination of repression, institutional co-optation, and ideological legitimation to maintain control over society (Frantz 2018; Dukalskis 2017; Dickson 2016, 3; Svolik 2012; Gandhi and Przeworski 2007). Despite a variety of tools used to stay in power, authoritarian regimes frequently face the dual challenge of preventing mass uprisings while keeping elite challengers at bay. In the first instance, the "problem of authoritarian control" requires autocrats to address threats of popular opposition. In the second instance, the "problem of authoritarian power-sharing" involves maintaining a ruling coalition – a close group of associates that can bolster the dictatorship and help ensure the regime's survival (Svolik 2012, 3–6; Bueno de Mesquita and Smith 2011). Although challenges from both above and below are addressed in this Element, a focus on state-society relations demands greater analytical attention to authoritarian control of the masses.

Through a combination of repression, co-optation, and legitimation, the North Korean regime has built a number of safeguards and mechanisms to prevent elite factions from challenging the Kim family dynasty. Potential challenges may arise from other institutions, most notably the military, the Workers' Party of Korea (WPK), and the bureaucracies (McEachern 2010). However, the North Korean leader heads all three institutions in an effort to "coup-proof" the regime. Much like leaders in China (Shirk 2007), Kim wears three different hats as the chairman of the State Affairs Commission; chairman of the WPK; and chair of the Central Military Commission. Institutional coup-proofing, aided by a healthy dose of fear and material benefits distributed to power players closest to the regime (the so-called selectorate), helps keep North Korean elites in line with the regime (Geddes et al. 2018; Bueno de Mesquita and Smith 2011).

The regime relies on a number of different strategies to keep the masses under control. Byman and Lind (2010, 47) discuss three strategies to keep the population at bay: restrictive social policies, the manipulation of ideas and information, and the use of severe force. First, restrictive social policies preempt the possibility of opposition while creating dependence on the regime. For instance, the regime developed the Public Distribution System (PDS) to allocate food rations according to one's *songbun* (social status), and thus keep the population in check. Loyal elites were rewarded greater rations, whereas members of the "hostile" class were given less and lower-quality food (Collins 2012, 57).[1] Although the PDS has ceased to function as an effective control mechanism since mass famine in the 1990s, close monitoring of all social interaction

---

[1] The PDS also regulated the distribution of clothes, housing, and daily commodities, in addition to food.

between individuals and within groups, has kept the population at bay (Byman and Lind 2010, 49).

The regime also controls and manipulates information to legitimize its rule and minimize dissent. This includes maintaining a cult of personality around North Korea's founder, Kim Il-sung, and his line of dynastic successors. North Koreans are constantly reminded of the greatness of their leaders, who are bestowed with honorific titles such as Eternal President, Supreme Leader, and Dear Leader. The state propaganda machine also promotes intense nationalism, evoking the threat of evil American imperialism and decadent South Korean capitalism to inculcate a martial spirit and strengthen state loyalty.

Meanwhile, the regime severely restricts access to outside information and limits contact between foreigners and North Koreans. Most North Koreans cannot connect to the internet, instead relying on North Korea's intranet system, which only allows North Koreans to see what the regime will permit. Radios and televisions are tuned to government-run stations. Evidence from defector surveys and interviews does suggest that the regime's grip on foreign information has somewhat weakened with the growth of a market economy. North Koreans with political connections and/or money are more readily able to cross into China and gain access to foreign radio broadcasts, movies, and South Korean dramas (Kretchun and Kim 2012; Baek 2016).[2] However, an elaborate surveillance system still makes it dangerous to communicate or exchange ideas that deviate from the party line. Neighbors who act as informants raise the risk of engaging in subversive activities.

Finally, severe and cruel punishment, including public executions, are used to suppress dissent. Through guilt by association, punishment for suspected dis-loyalty may include imprisonment of additional family members of up to three generations (Collins 2012, 7). In sum, the combination of restrictive social policies, ideological indoctrination, information control, surveillance, and vio-lence have enabled the Kim family to stay in power for over seven decades.

1.2 Markets in North Korea

Although the state dominates every aspect of society in North Korea, one significant development that has affected state-society relations since the late 1990s has been the rise of informal markets. A more detailed analysis of rising markets is offered in Section 3, but for now it suffices to state that the growth of the informal economy may represent the single most significant change in North

---

[2] On the efficacy of foreign broadcasts, Kern and Hainmueller (2017) have found that foreign radio broadcasts from West Germany to East Germany had the opposite of their intended effect in that they provided more support for the East German regime.

Korea in the past three decades. Despite Kim Jong-un's aspiration to develop North Korea into a "socialist civilization" (*Rodong Sinmun* 2013, 2019), North Koreans increasingly rely on income earned from markets rather than the formal command economy for their livelihood (Kim 2017, 119; Haggard and Noland 2011).

Unable to do away with markets, and also recognizing the benefits of marketization (including the global trade of illicit and sanctioned goods) as an important source of revenue, the regime is attempting to regulate rather than completely shut down market activity. Markets now constitute an important part of everyday life in North Korea. In the short run, markets have forced the state to make policy adjustments including the decentralization of the command economy, even as it continues to maintain tight control over social and political life.

The longer term effects of marketization on state-society relations, not to mention the North Korean economy itself, remain unclear given the number of constraints and contingencies that factor into the regime's decision making. For instance, the trifecta of international sanctions, the COVID-19 pandemic, and a powerful typhoon in 2020 wreaked havoc on the economy, and likely everyday life in North Korea, forcing the regime to tighten market control and limit the flow of foreign currency (Wertz 2020; Babson 2020; Silberstein 2020b). Domestic political constraints, including the potential rise of elite challengers, and relations with external actors such as the United States, China, South Korea, and the United Nations, will also affect the regime's ability to pursue more fundamental market reforms and economic development.

Contingencies and constraints (and opportunities) notwithstanding, the rapid rise of marketization in North Korea has led to speculation about societal change (Dukalskis and Joo 2020; Yeo 2020; Smith 2015; David-West 2013). In particular, the spontaneous development of market activities – what Haggard and Noland (2007, 147) refer to as "marketization from below" – suggests a change in the nature of the relationship between state and society (Daily NK 2017, 5). To what degree the regime maintains control over markets, and the implications of bottom-up marketization, is debatable (Yeo 2020; Dukalskis 2016). Drawing on defector surveys, several studies indicate that most North Koreans participate in some form of market activity, whether as consumers or producers (IPUS 2020; Kim 2017; Daily NK 2017). North Koreans increasingly rely on markets, not the socialist state, to make ends meet. Juxtaposing the gap between the promises and ideology of the socialist state with the reality of markets and the "entrepreneurial spirit" (Hastings 2016) of North Koreans thus raises an important question about the legitimacy of the regime and greater autonomy for society.

1.3 North Korean Society

Civil society, at least as conventionally understood (i.e. organized social life that is "voluntary, self-generating, self-supporting, and autonomous from the state"),[3] may not exist yet in North Korea. However, the absence of organized life independent of the state does not mean that shifts in state-society relations cannot occur. I briefly consider three different perspectives on civil society: as a public sphere, as associational life and networks of trust, and as a source of resistance. There is significant overlap across all three, but an emphasis here is placed on the public sphere and trust networks.[4]

Civil society as a concept is difficult to pinpoint as its meaning has varied over time and place and across different intellectual traditions (Alagappa 2004, 26). It can refer to voluntary associations, nongovernmental organizations (NGOs), civic groups, and social movements. Sometimes civil society complements the state by providing public service, contributing to good governance, and acting as an independent "watchdog" against state authority. In other instances, civil society is in opposition to the state, as witnessed by frequent protests and social movements against governments.[5] Unfortunately, none of these different manifestations of civil society fully exist in North Korea. However, this reality should not deter us from exploring the dynamic relationship between markets, state, and society in North Korea.

1.3.1 Public Sphere

I look at civil society as part of the (nonstate) public sphere. Civil society exists largely in the public realm, thus excluding individual and family life as well as "inward-looking group activity" related to recreation and entertainment (Diamond 1994, 4). Yet, some scholars explicitly or implicitly include family or private gatherings in their conceptualization of civil society (Smith 2015, 213; Bendix, Bendix, and Furniss 1987, 14).[6] Others place civil society somewhere between the private and public sphere. As Marc Howard (2003, 1) states

---

[3] This definition draws from Larry Diamond's (1994, 5) conception of civil society.

[4] This is for both pragmatic and theoretical reasons. Pragmatically, it is difficult to evaluate empirically whether any associational life or opposition movements exist in North Korea. Theoretically, in an illiberal environment, the development of a public sphere may be analytically prior to the rise of oppositional movements.

[5] Foley and Edwards (1996, 39) distinguish between these two conceptions of civil society as "civil society I" in which habits of association and horizontal networks foster patterns of civility, and "civil society II," which emphasizes a "sphere of action that is independent of the state" capable of organizing resistance to tyranny.

[6] As Smith (2015, 213) states, in North Korea, "one unanticipated effect of marketization was the rise of the family as the nexus of economic and associational life and the gradual displacement of collectivist, state-led priorities from private life."

in his study of civil society in postcommunist Europe, civil society is conceived "as a crucial part of the public space between the state and the family."

Describing eighteenth-century Europe, Jürgen Habermas (1991, 30) remarks that "the private sphere comprised civil society in the narrower sense ... imbedded in it was the family with its interior domain." As Habermas (1991, 27) argues, the public sphere "may be conceived above all as the sphere of private people come together as a public." Under this view, the strength and vitality of civil society is not measured by the number of NGOs or the size and efficacy of mass mobilization, but by the vitality of an arena for contestation where ideas and discourse are debated (Edwards 2009, 8). In this Element, I examine the exchange of ideas and discourse that occurs among private actors and in the public space. It is at the intersection of the private and public realm where civil society is most likely to develop (see Figure 1). Thus civil society is conceptualized more as a space that can expand or contract over time rather than as an actor.

1.3.2 Trust Networks and Associational Life

Civil society as embodied in associational life is less likely to exist in an autocratic state such as North Korea. Although collective organizations such as the youth league or women's union may organize individuals to "volunteer" for public works projects (e.g. village beautification projects or performances during national celebrations), these groups exist to indoctrinate citizens and supply the regime with free mass labor. However, increasing marketization may also help encourage the

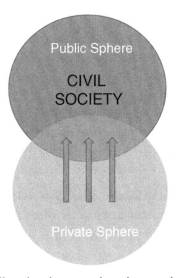

Figure 1 Civil society between the private and public sphere

formation of associational life through the development of social capital and trust.[7] As Putnam (1993, 171–172) argues, "social trust in complex modern settings can arise from norms of reciprocity and networks of civic engagement ... an effective norm of generalized reciprocity is likely to be associated with dense networks of social exchange ... Conversely, repeated exchange over a period of time tends to encourage the development of a norm of generalized reciprocity."

Although there are official, legalized markets in North Korea, a variety of black markets or informal markets also operate in North Korea. Low-level entrepreneurs such as street vendors may sell vegetables or cheap consumer goods in local currency, while wealthy business owners may build connections with party officials and managers of state-owned companies to obtain access to goods in China and secure transportation routes in North Korea. By offering state officials a cut of their profits, wealthier entrepreneurs enable their supply chains to flow uninterrupted. Needless to say, market participants must build a certain modicum of trust with others to survive in a politically uncertain, information-scarce environment.

Trust is built over time through repeated interaction, past experiences, and reputation. As Coleman (1990, 109) argues, "the reputation for trustworthiness is of central importance ... because that reputation is quickly communicated among all those on whom the trustee depends for future business, that is, for future placement of trust." Market participants may retaliate against cheaters, either individually or collectively, by damaging their reputation and ceasing to buy (or sell) from an individual. Hence, market rules or norms may develop, informing participants what behavior is (un)acceptable in the markets to protect the functioning of the wider market (Hastings et al. 2021, 36). Mutually beneficial relations, even if motivated by profit, may also generate social capital as "networks, norms, and trust" enable participants to "act together more effectively to pursue shared interests" (Jackman and Miller 1998, 49).

Civic engagement – at least that which is not in obligation to or coerced by the state – may be in short supply in North Korea. However, if North Korean markets create opportunities for social exchange, which in turn generate networks of trust apart from the state, we may begin to see a shift in state-society relations as trust, social capital, and reciprocity expand from the private to the public sphere.

1.3.3 Resistance and Opposition

Finally, some scholars are inclined to define civil society as "a sphere of action that is independent of the state and capable of energizing resistance against

---

[7] Putnam describes social capital as features of social organization such as trust, norms, and networks that can improve the efficiency of society by facilitating coordinated action (Putnam 1993, 167).

tyranny" (Foley and Edwards 1996, 38).[8] Those who see the rise of civil society as a means of challenging an authoritarian state or advancing regime change adopt this conception of civil society. The prospects of a bottom-up revolt in North Korea, however, appear remote (Cha and Anderson 2012; Lee 2012). Although not explored here, the possibility of collective action and organized resistance against the state nevertheless remains a tempting speculation, especially if the perceived gap between state and society widens.[9]

As implied above, most definitions of civil society tend to delineate state from society. In practice, however, the line between state and society is often blurred. While in many Western, democratic societies a dense network of voluntary associations and civic groups does operate independently of the state, in corporatist or social democratic states such as Germany or Sweden, respectively, organizations such as trade unions or employee associations may be integrated with the state. As Taylor (1990, 96) argues, "what occurs is an interweaving of society and government to the point where the distinction no longer expresses an important difference in the basis of power or the dynamics of policy-making." Even in authoritarian regimes, states do not necessarily exist in opposition to society in that civic organizations may work in conjunction with the state to provide public goods (Teets 2014). Where society ends and the state begins may thus vary across different polities and political systems.

These different conceptions of civil society have a significant impact on how we understand shifting state-society relations. If one rigidly defines the realm of society as wholly independent from the state, then the prospect for civil society's development in an authoritarian state such as North Korea is indeed slim given the regime's heavy intervention in public life. However, by relaxing the boundaries between state and society, the potential for societal change looks more promising. Developments such as the growth of private networks that include ties to state officials in informal markets, or a gathering of friends and family watching the latest South Korean drama as the neighborhood watch leader turns a blind eye, may be more indicative of changing state-society relations.

1.3.4 Markets and Society

Although political scientists tend to focus on the relationship between state and society, earlier studies elaborated on the important role of markets in the

---

[8] This view is found in the democratic transition literature. See Kim 2000; Linz and Stepan 1996; Ekiert 1997.

[9] North Koreans do protest against the regime on rare occasions as witnessed in the aftermath of the regime's 2009 currency reform debacle. See Lankov 2013, 129–31.

development of state-society relations. Hegel defined civil society as a sphere of market relations "regulated by civil law, intervening between the family and the state" (Alagappa 2004, 27).[10] Markets provide the material basis for society's independence from the state, with an autonomous economy serving as an "essential precondition for the conceptual differentiation of civil society from the state" (Schwartz 2003, 31). This process is further explained by Alagappa (2004, 27) who states, "With the development of the commercial state in eighteenth-century Europe, civil society, conceived essentially as a market-organized sphere of production and competition, came to be viewed as a distinct, legally protected public realm, separate from family and state."

Jürgen Habermas (1991) also identified the role of markets in the formation of a public sphere. The growth of trade and commerce in eighteenth-century Europe led to the development of taverns, salons, and coffee houses along commercial trade routes. This in turn provided space where information about goods and prices, along with other news, ideas, and gossip of the day might be exchanged – thus giving rise to a bourgeois public (Habermas 1991, 30). These earlier insights linking markets to the development of civil society are worth considering when thinking about the rise of markets in authoritarian spaces.

1.4 Legitimacy, Ideology, and the Public Sphere

Coercion and fear are costly tools to maintain control over society, and few (if any) political regimes can survive long term on the basis of repression and co-optation alone (von Haldenwang 2017, 271). Dictators therefore rely on ideology to legitimate their rule. To this end, regime ideology almost always extolls the virtues of its leaders and their accomplishments. In personalist dictatorships, the legitimacy of a single leader is tantamount to the legitimacy of the entire political system as "the leader has been amalgamated with the ideas of country, nation, and state" (Frank and Park 2012, 34).

North Korea is no different in this respect; legitimacy and ideology remain central to state-society relations. The regime's adoption of *juche* (roughly translated as self-reliance) ideology flows from the ideas and leadership of Kim Il-sung. *Juche* has been described as "expressions of North Korean particularism over supposedly more universalistic Marxism-Leninism" (Shin 2006, 90). It applies to "all areas of political, economic, and social activity" (Armstrong 2013) and reinforces the legitimacy of the Kim family's "*Baekdu* revolutionary bloodline" (Young 2020).

---

[10] However, Hegel believed that markets and private interests might occasionally lead to instability within civil society, requiring the state to then guide and give order to society. See Alagappa 2004, 27.

Personalist dictators reinforce their legitimacy through various means that either shore up or prevent subjects from deviating from the regime's official ideology, which dominates the authoritarian public sphere (Huang 2018; Dukalskis 2017).[11] First, dictators indoctrinate the population with a "totalitarian ideology" that seeks to "offer total explanation of the past, the total knowledge of the present, and the reliable prediction of the future" (Arendt 1951, quoted in Dukalskis and Gerschewski 2017, 252). Totalitarian ideologies present themselves as logical entities, even if they deviate significantly from empirical reality (Dukalskis and Gerschewski 2017, 252).

Second, the regime actively mobilizes its citizens in support of its leaders and its (revolutionary) ideology. As in other communist regimes, North Koreans are constantly mobilized to participate in mass celebrations, mass games, and mass public works that not only project loyalty to the regime to domestic and foreign audiences but also display the regime's power (Ekiert et al. 2020). Paradoxically, such active mobilization leads to passivity on the part of citizens as the regime's ideology "clutters public space with monotonous slogans and empty gestures, which tire the minds and bodies of producers and consumers alike" (Wedeen 2015, 6). The public display of regime power acts as a deterrent against potential opposition while discrediting alternative ideas (Dukalskis and Gerschewski 2017, 259).

Third, legitimacy is tied to economic performance regarding people's access to everyday material goods, public services, and other tangible outputs that signify the "success" of the regime (Von Haldenwang 2017, 276; Frank and Park 2012). Fourth, external threats, whether real or constructed, and the establishment of the garrison state, help reinforce a regime's legitimacy. By extension, a powerful military and aggressive foreign policy, including the possession of nuclear weapons, can serve to strengthen nationalist ideology. Finally, information control and censorship, although not a direct source of legitimacy, functions as a necessary condition for sustaining autocratic rulers. Censorship strengthens a regime's legitimation claims while silencing the voices of its critics (Dukalskis and Gerschewski 2017, 261).

If the basis of authoritarian legitimacy rests on a combination of totalitarian ideology, an actively mobilized but passive citizenry, political-economic performance, external threats, and information control, then the absence or weakening of any of these features should contribute to regime instability. When faced with declining legitimacy and weakening ideology, autocrats must

---

[11] Mechanisms of authoritarian legitimation draw from and expand on the four offered by Dukalskis and Gerschewski (2017, 253–55): ideological legitimation; passive legitimation; performance-based legitimation; and democratic procedural legitimation. Dukalskis (2017) offers more specific legitimation mechanisms adopted by the North Korean regime.

increase repression or find new ways to co-opt citizens. For instance, several Soviet bloc regimes facing economic crisis in the 1980s initiated a series of ideological, economic, and institutional reforms to "counteract the drops in both elite and popular support that occur when economic crisis and ideological erosion set in" (Dimitrov 2013, 33). Institutional adaptation is seen as an effort to shore up legitimacy in support of regime survival. Although communist parties in Eastern Europe were ultimately unsuccessful in adapting their institutions and ideology to the shifting political-economic environment, those in China and Vietnam remained resilient, in part by incorporating marketization as a part of their new ideology (Dickson 2016). In effect, regime elites replaced Marxism-Leninism with marketization and nationalism as the new basis for regime ideology (Dimitrov 2013, 25).

When marketization and economic reforms are initiated by the socialist state, the regime still has some control over the framing of markets and its incorporation into the regime's ideology. However, if the state fails to make adaptive institutional or ideational changes to capture markets – even as market forces hollow out the socialist economy – the regime is placed in a more precarious position. Contradictions emerge as state actors become dependent on private entrepreneurs for survival rather than the other way around. When market forces are driven from below, the regime must constantly work to co-opt practices and behavior that remain fundamentally at odds with the regime's core ideology.

The rise of markets may erode state legitimacy and authority in at least three ways. First, society's dependence on markets rather than the state for survival may lead North Koreans to question the regime's legitimacy. As Smith (2015, 212) argues, the WPK's participation in and support for market activity may be seen as contradicting the official state line. In doing so, the regime (and party) "ceased to act as a well-functioning, reliable transmission belt for ideological education and revolutionary discipline."

Second, although a system of bribery and corruption can "grease the wheels" of markets and strengthen ties between state officials and private entrepreneurs, over time, corruption can also undermine state authority. The willingness of state bureaucrats and economic managers to participate in markets makes it more difficult for the regime to enforce policies that might curtail marketization. Over time, market participants, and the population more generally, may fear the regime less (at least as it pertains to market activity) as state officials tolerate subversive behavior. For these reasons, the Kim family has periodically launched anticorruption campaigns resulting in the imprisonment, and in some extreme cases execution, of corrupt officials and wealthy business owners.

Third, markets and trade networks offer North Koreans greater access to goods, ideas, and information about the outside world, allowing them to verify the gap between the regime's rhetoric and reality. Information campaigns led by human rights activists, and interactions with foreigners through humanitarian, development, and other people-to-people networks that encourage knowledge sharing and the exchange of ideas also expose North Koreans to the outside world (Yeo and Chubb 2018; Baek 2016; Yeo 2017). Moreover, marketization whether at the level of the *jangmadang*[12] and general markets or among state-owned enterprise (SOE) managers and party elites near the top has led to informal trust networks that extend beyond family or community ties.

Taken together, the growth of markets, as well as participation in and access to the informal economy, may weaken the authoritarian public sphere. As legitimacy erodes, the gap between private and public thoughts about the regime may widen. Critical views about the regime may also spread (Joo 2014; Kuran 1991). Addressing the doublespeak that existed in communist countries in Eastern Europe, Vladimir Tismaneanu (2013, 89–90) states, "Ironically, ideological imperialism resulted in a simulacrum of faith, which was merely a camouflage for the ideological vacuum. At the moment this imposture was exposed, the whole castle would fall apart ... these systems experienced a perpetual ideological crisis: their promises had long lost any credibility."

In short, the rise and expansion of markets alters state-society relations by undermining the regime's legitimating strategies and by chipping away at the authoritarian public sphere. Furthermore, marketization has created different networks of relationships among North Koreans that may serve as a conduit for an emerging semipublic sphere (particularly within the informal market space) where ideas and information are exchanged. Although these networks may still rely on the state for permission to conduct business, they have helped shift economic power away from states to private actors who have amassed large amounts of capital, credit, and finance. This shift does not necessarily mean that market actors will push for economic and eventual political reforms, especially if market activity is prescribed within the limits of what the state deems acceptable (Daily NK 2017). Nor should one make teleological assumptions that an emerging public sphere, even one more critical of the regime, will inspire mass mobilization, elite defections, or political change. Although some may see private entrepreneurs as agents of change paving the way for political reform, the reality may prove quite different: in the case of China, capitalists, rather than promote political change, have become an important base of support for the party (Dickson 2007, 827; Tsai 2007).

---

[12] *Jangmadang* literally translates to "market grounds" and is used to describe local markets, including those operating unofficially.

Nevertheless, the above theoretical discussion on rising markets, civil society, and regime legitimacy suggests how state-society relations might evolve in a direction more conducive to civil society development in North Korea. However, the process is highly contingent on a set of domestic and international factors. Among them, one key factor rests with the regime's ability (or failure) to capture market dynamics and co-opt market actors. The inability to incorporate markets into the regime's official discourse will further erode the regime's legitimacy while strengthening market-based horizontal networks, thus creating more space for a public sphere.

1.5 Data and Methods

Due to the challenge of direct access to North Korea, social scientists have relied on surveys and interviews with the North Korean defector population to glean insights into North Korea (Dukalskis and Joo 2020; Haggard and Noland 2018, 2011, 2007; Kim 2017; Dalton et al. 2017; Fahy 2015; Choi 2013). My research makes use of existing survey data with North Korean defectors,[13] most notably the Institute for Peace and Unification Studies (IPUS) annual North Korean defector survey published through their Unification Perception Survey series.[14]

However, as others have noted (Song and Denney 2019), North Korean defectors are not representative of the broader North Korean population, nor are they an unbiased sample. Around 75 percent of the nearly 34,000 defectors (as of 2020) in South Korea hail from just two provinces along the Sino-North Korea border: North Hamgyong and Ryanggang provinces. The defectors are also overwhelmingly female (about 72 percent).[15] Although researchers have attempted to reduce hindsight bias by interviewing defectors within one year after their defection, biases cannot be eliminated altogether from an arguably self-selected sample: preexisting characteristics and attitudes may have made

---

[13] I use the term "defector" as this appears to be the most common English term used among political scientists to describe North Koreans who have left (or escaped) North Korea and permanently reside in another country. The South Korean Ministry of Unification also continues to use the term "defector" in English translations of its official policy, even though it has adopted the term *italjumin*, which translates to "residents who have escaped or defected from North Korea." For additional discussion, see Hur 2020; Lankov 2006.

[14] For an archive of survey reports and data including original questions (in Korean), see "Unification Ceremony Survey," Institute for Peace and Unification Studies, Seoul National University, https://ipus.snu.ac.kr/blog/archives/research_cat/unification_perception-survey and also annual reports on "North Korean social change" at https://ipus.snu.ac.kr/blog/archives/research_cat/nksurvey.

[15] For annually updated statistics on North Korean defectors in South Korea, see "Policy on North Korean Defectors," South-North Relations, Ministry of Unification, Republic of Korea, www.unikorea.go.kr/eng_unikorea/relations/statistics/defectors/.

defectors more prone to defect compared with the broader North Korean population. As such, defector surveys and interviews cannot be taken as definitive.

The solution for researchers is not to avoid defector-based evidence, which to date has provided invaluable information about North Korea and offers the most direct account of everyday life in North Korea, but to collect data using a variety of sources and methods. Taken in conjunction with other pieces of evidence, defector surveys and interviews may offer reasonable conjectures about the effects of markets on state-society relations (Yeo 2020). This Element thus builds on several recent studies in English and in Korean that address the rise of markets and its implications for North Korea (Lee 2018; Park et al. 2018; Cha and Collins 2018; NK Daily 2017; Kim 2017; Smith 2015). Insights are also drawn from formal interviews and informal discussions with field-workers in the development, business, and humanitarian space who regularly work and/or reside in North Korea, and discussions with policy experts with extensive, in-country knowledge of North Korea.[16] I also interviewed North Korean defectors affiliated with defector-run organizations that maintain regular contact with those inside North Korea to examine whether the mechanisms outlined in the theoretical framework actually operate in practice.

Although official North Korean sources include their own inherent biases, news sources such as the *Rodong Sinmun* and Korea Central News Agency (KCNA) reports, as well as publications produced by the government-run Foreign Languages Publishing House, such as the *Pyongyang Times*, *Foreign Trade*, and *Korea Today*, also offer insights into North Korean economy and society. Data is also culled and analyzed in research outlets dedicated to information on North Korea such as the NK Pro database and 38 North – all resources I use to understand North Korean state, society, and markets. In sum, although data on North Korea remains limited, by triangulating defector surveys with existing data on North Korea's economy and interviews with international field-workers and experts who reside in or travel extensively to North Korea, researchers can provide a reasonably informed analysis on market growth and its implications for social and political change (Yeo 2020).

2 Authority, Legitimacy, and the Totalitarian State

These are not mere excesses of the State; they are essential components of a political system that has moved far from the ideals on which it claims to be

---

[16] Many of these connections were made possible through my affiliation with the National Committee for North Korea, and also contacts with faith-based organizations involved in capacity-building projects in North Korea.

founded. The gravity, scale and nature of these violations reveal a State that does not have any parallel in the contemporary world. Political scientists of the twentieth century characterized this type of political organization as a totalitarian state.

–United Nations Commission of Inquiry (UNCOI 2014, 15)

The effect of the regime's power is manifest in the active compliance of mobilized citizens, but also in citizens' passive compliance, in the cynical apathy of those who obey because they have become habituated to the cult or in order to be left in peace.

–Lisa Wedeen (2015, 147)

There was nothing inherent to the northern half of the Korean Peninsula in August 1945 that would suggest its rapid descent into a totalitarian state, seeking to "dominate every aspect of its citizens' lives and terrorize them from within" (UNCOI 2014, 15). In fact, in the immediate aftermath of Korean liberation from Japan (1945–1946), it was the northern half of Korea, not the southern half, that more closely reflected the grassroots ideals of representative democracy through the spread of self-governing people's committees. The people's committees provided "substantial autonomy and space for self-governance" and served as the basis for an independent Korea (Kim 2013, 5).[17] People's committees and party chapters formed within villages, suggesting that the North Korean Revolution[18] was not simply led from the top by one individual. Rather, as historian Suzy Kim (2013, 14) argues, it was "everyday life" that became the "primary site of political struggle and the single most important arena for experiencing the revolution in progress."

Unfortunately, grassroots independent governance was short-lived, quickly falling casualty to brewing Cold War geopolitics and internal politicking among rival nationalist leaders and communist factions. By August 1946, Kim Il-sung and the North Korean Workers' Party had emerged to dominate politics and centralize authority – including that of the people's committees, which were absorbed rather than disbanded by the WPK (Cumings 1997, 228). Nationalist and Christian political figures were arrested or purged. With Soviet support, Kim Il-sung was named premier of the newly proclaimed North Korean state on September 9, 1948. Rather than shape North Korea into the mold of other Soviet satellites, however, the regime instead transformed society "to promote a totalitarian dictatorship where only the Supreme Leader, the Kim family, and the WPK are to be respected and praised" (Collins 2018, ix).

---

[17] People's committees also appeared in the South, but were eyed suspiciously as left leaning and quickly suppressed by the US military government.

[18] The North Korean Revolution describes North Korea's political-economic transformation from a Japanese colonial-capitalist state to a socialist society.

This section focuses on the North Korean state and its ideological and institutional foundations. Similar to other autocratic regimes, North Korea employs a combination of coercion, co-optation, and legitimation to maintain control over its population. The distinctiveness of North Korea's brand of authoritarianism may therefore be one of degree rather than kind. Restrictive social policies, severe repression, and intense ideological indoctrination have enabled the state to penetrate deep into society to a degree unparalleled by most other authoritarian states. This penetration is intensely physical and psychological and extends across the entire political, economic, and social spectrum.

Rather than outline every authoritarian tool used to maintain autocratic control in North Korea, I focus on the crux of the Kim family's control over the North Korean people: its command over the authoritarian public sphere (Dukalskis 2017) and its ability to elicit compliance through "enforced participation in rituals of obeisance" (Wedeen 2015, 6). Repression and violence tend to capture the most attention when describing North Korean authoritarianism. However, such tactics are often a means to a larger end. Coercive institutions such as the secret police and prison camps are intended to prevent ideological deviation and remind the North Korean people of the virtues of the regime and its ideology. This is not to argue that repression, coercion, co-optation, or institutional coup-proofing matter any less in sustaining North Korea's authoritarian rule than ideology. To emphasize the importance of legitimacy and compliance as an element of authoritarian control, however, this section gives greater attention to the regime's use of ideology, propaganda, and other legitimation strategies.

2.1 The Rise of the Personalist Dictatorship

Among the different types of authoritarian regimes, North Korea is best described as a personalist dictatorship (Song and Wright 2018), in which near absolute power is held by a single leader who pushes the regime towards greater personalization to secure political (and military) control (Geddes et al. 2018; Kendall-Taylor et al. 2017). The leader controls key political appointments, pronounces major policy directives, and limits the ruling class to family members and loyal allies (Frantz 2018, 77).

The sequence and timing of personalization is important. As political scientist Erica Frantz (2018, 49) finds, in most instances, the process of personalization "often occurs during the first few years after the regime seizes power, when it is still uncertain what the rules of the game will be." Kim Il-sung had the good fortune of receiving support from two foreign powers, the Soviet Union and China, which enabled him to consolidate power over the military at the outset of his rule (Song and Wright 2018, 175). Scholars of authoritarian politics have also found that the personalization of power in dictatorships leads to an increase in repression (Frantz et al. 2020). In North Korea's case, Kim Il-sung wasted no time in eliminating rivals and elevating family members and loyalists, particularly among his former Manchurian guerrilla comrades. Although the process of stamping out rivals began even prior to the Korean War, in the postconflict period between 1953 and 1957, Kim eliminated other rival communist factions. He then widened the hunt to remove anyone suspected of disloyalty, leading to 100,000 arrests and 2,500 executions between 1957 and 1959 (Seth 2016, 368).

During an era when de-Stalinization in the Soviet Union encouraged a shift away from strongman rule, Kim in contrast built his own personality-cult regime. Titles such as Great Leader, Sun of the Nation, and the Ever-Victorious General were bestowed upon Kim. Regime propagandists attributed a long list of impossible feats to the Great Leader, embellishing or altering history to highlight Kim's nationalist and anti-imperial credentials. For instance, Kim is credited with establishing Korean communism at age fourteen when he founded the Anti-Imperialist Union (Lankov 2013a, 52) and of playing an outsized role in Japan's defeat in World War II (Fifield 2019, 17). Ideological indoctrination also constituted a key portion of North Korea's education curriculum with the most important school subjects focusing on the revolutionary history of the Kim family (Lankov 2013a, 66).

The deification of North Korea's leaders should be understood in the context of Kim's efforts to personalize the regime. Sacred portraits of North Korea's father and son (and now grandson) adorn every house, classroom, and office in North Korea. A set of complex regulations instruct North Koreans (and foreigners) on how portraits of the Great Leader and Dear Leader should be maintained, respected, and preserved. Tourists are reminded to never cover or block the images of the leader when taking photos. Statues of the Great Leader adorn the country and form a central role during rituals performed on major holidays. For example, North Koreans pay respects to their leaders by offering a deep bow and laying flowers at the feet of Kim Il-sung's towering statue.

Seeking greater autonomy from China and Russia, the regime promoted its own ideology of *juche* rather than existing Marxist-Leninist or Maoist ideologies. The term *juche*[19] first appeared in a 1955 address to the WPK by Kim Il-sung, and would continue to develop as a core element of state ideology as articulated in the words and speeches of the Great Leader throughout the 1960s (Hassig and Oh 2015, 123). *Juche* thus reinforces the personality cult of the

---

[19]   Lankov (2013a, 62) has translated the term as "self-importance" or "self-significance." Hassig and Oh (2015, 123) have also argued that *juche* instills a sense of national pride.

Eternal Leader and his descendants, and "underpin(s) the regime's justifica-tion for rule over and control of the North Korean populace" (Collins 2019, 35). *Juche* and "our-style socialism" was the regime's attempt to legitimize an "incomplete nation-state" through national identity formation by pinning Korea's postcolonial experience to its founding father (Armstrong 2013, 103).

2.2 Mobilizing the Masses

A focus on the repressive nature of the North Korean state leaves the impression that North Koreans were all violently coerced to accept the Kim regime. While repression and violence were certainly important tools for maintaining loyalty and social control, North Koreans had reason to grant legitimacy to Kim Il-sung. The brewing Cold War and rising tensions across the 38th parallel resulted in the rapid centralization and militarization of state power in the late 1940s. This included mobilizing and training thousands of youth league members and students in preparation for conflict. During the Korean War, US bombers had leveled virtually every city in North Korea, and North Koreans experienced a disproportionately higher number of casualties than South Korea. For sure, the Kim regime exploited the threat of US imperialism, but in the war's aftermath, North Koreans had every reason to support a militarized security state.

From utter destruction, North Koreans, under the direction of Kim, managed to quickly rebuild their economy in the 1950s. Industrial production returned to prewar levels following the regime's three-year economic plan (1954–1956). This was followed by a five-year plan (1957–1961) that coincided with the "Chollima movement"[20] as work teams competed to outproduce one another in exceeding their daily quotas (Seth 2016, 366). The state organized campaigns such as the "Movement to See the Early Morning Stars" or devised slogans including "One Stretch After One Thousand Shovels" to motivate laborers and farmers to maximize productivity by beginning work before the crack of dawn and reducing the number of break periods during the day (Seth 2016, 366).

Kim's five-year plan, oriented towards heavy industry and fueled by Soviet aid, helped triple industrial output from 1956 to 1960 (Seth 2016, 365). However, the regime's economic success rested on the backs of its workers. Rapid development in the 1950s and the early 1960s thus relied on the mobil-ization of local production units. At the same time, nationalist mobilization and rapid industrialization helped further consolidate Kim Il-sung's legitimacy among the masses. Raised living standards and widespread achievements in

---

[20] Chollima is a mythical horse capable of galloping hundreds of miles a day, thus implying endurance.

mass education also reinforced Kim's own cult of personality by reflecting the Great Father's love and care for his people. According to the regime, Kim's followers responded in true neo-Confucian fashion by reciprocating a spirit of obedience, respect, and filial piety (Cumings 1997, 408).

2.3 Authoritarian Tools and Strategies

By the 1960s, Kim Il-sung had eliminated communist rivals at the top. The mobilization of the masses – aided by economic nationalism and development progress, and justified by the constant state of war in the aftermath of the Korean War – helped solidify Kim's legitimacy. To further cultivate the cult of personality and maintain authoritarian control, the regime resorted to several strategies.

2.3.1 Ideology and Information Control

The North Korean state is undoubtedly capable of inflicting brutal physical violence against its people. However, ideological indoctrination and the legitimation of authority have been key to the Supreme Leader's survival. As Andrei Lankov (2013a, 45) argues, the regime focuses more on "prevention of ideological deviation rather than open state terror." Prison camps and mutual surveillance are tools used to maintain ideological conformity. The regime's heavy use of rhetoric and symbols, including significant investment in mass spectacles such as the *Arirang* Mass Games and public anniversaries commemorating the Great Leader, have been instrumental in maintaining compliance (but not always loyalty as discussed later).

Hassig and Oh (2015, 122) describe the Kim regime as "inordinately proud of its ideology." To quote from the *Rodong Sinmun*, the offical newspaper of the WPK, "Some countries are known for their economic prosperity and others for military strength … But our country is the only country known for its ideological power" (quoted in Hassig and Oh 2015, 122). To reinforce *juche* ideology and Kim Il-sung's rule (if not deity) as Supreme Ruler, the regime adopted the "Ten Principles to Safeguard the Party's Unitary Ideology System" in 1974. The first principle states "All must struggle whole-heartedly to remake the entire society into Kim Il-sung/Kim Jong-Il-ism." The fourth principle declares that "All must absolutely arm themselves with revolutionary ideology of Great Leader Kim Il-sung and Dear Leader Kim Jong Il, and the Party's lines and policies, which are the specifics of that ideology" (quoted in Kim et al. 2019, 184). As guidelines that "ideologically govern the North Korean system," the Ten Principles carry greater authority than even the North Korean constitution (Kim et al. 2019, 183). In 2013, the regime revised the Ten Principles to focus on the leadership of Kim Jong-un. The revisions called on the party to strengthen its "unified ideological resolve and revolutionary unity around the leader" and "tighten ideological control over the population" (Kim et al. 2019, 183).

One need not look far to see the role of ideology and legitimation in North Korean politics and society. Signs and banners with ideological slogans adorn streets and buildings in Pyongyang, not to mention the myriad of monuments and museums memorializing the Kim family and their achievements. North Korea's constitution calls for a free press, but news and media do little more than act as a government mouthpiece. In fact, the state describes its own press as "a sharp ideological weapon dedicated to staunchly safeguarding and defending the leader" with the intent to "dye the whole society one color, the color of the revolutionary ideology of the Great Leader" (KCNA February 12, 2004; quoted in Hassig and Oh 2015, 95).

The state education curriculum also injects a heavy dose of political ideology idolizing the Kim family. Once lauded for its education system in the 1950s and 1960s, as Kim's personality cult developed over time "studies of the Kim family began to crowd out standard academic subjects" (Hassig and Oh 2015, 107). Article 43 of the North Korean constitution states that socialist pedagogy is intended to "raise the younger generation as resolute revolutionaries who wage struggles for the society and people and as new *juche*-type people" (quoted in Hassig and Oh 2015, 107). The curriculum includes five categories: "1) the greatness of the WPK and Supreme Leader, 2) *juche* ideology, 3) party policies, 4) the revolutionary tradition, and 5) revolutionary and communist education" (Kim et al. 2019, 402). Regular academic subjects are infused with political ideology and praise for the Kim family. For example, a second grade math textbook will include the following type of question: "During the Fatherland Liberation War [North Korea's official name for the Korean War] the brave uncles of Korean People's Army killed 265 American Imperial bastards in the first battle. In the second battle they killed 70 more bastards than they had in the first battle. How many bastards did they kill in the second battle?" (Lankov 2013a, 60).

All North Koreans are required to participate in "organizational life" meetings (or *jojik saenghwal*) through membership in associations that serve the "dual purpose of surveillance and indoctrination" (Lankov et al. 2012, 193). At age fourteen, North Koreans are expected to join party youth organizations (e.g. Young Pioneers). A few select North Koreans will eventually join the WPK. The majority who do not will remain in the youth organization until the age of thirty, or join a trade, agriculture, or other occupation-based union. Women outside of the formal economic sector join the women's union (Lankov 2013a,

40). Each week, respective organizations hold two indoctrination sessions comprised of lectures and political study sessions that address current political events, extol the virtues of the Supreme Leader, and discuss the evil nature of American imperialism (Lankov et al. 2012, 202). Through group-based indoctrination sessions, North Koreans are socialized (or programmed) to recite key slogans, speeches, and political messages.

In addition to the indoctrination sessions, a third meeting is devoted to self-criticism, or sometimes referred to as *saenghwal chonghwa* (life-review session). In small cell groups, participants publicly confess to shortcomings committed since their last meeting. Each participant is then criticized in turn by another member of the same cell. As stated in the party's Ten Principles of Unitary Ideology, North Koreans must "Participate without absence in more than two hours of study groups, lectures and collective studies devoted to revolutionary ideas of Great Leader Comrade Kim Il-sung, ensure discipline for these studies and make these studies a habitual part of daily life" (quoted in Williams 2019, 22). Even if the sessions are more performative than substantive, and North Koreans are careful not to overly criticize others or admit wrongdoing for any offenses leading to severe punishment, regular self-criticism keeps North Koreans in line with regime ideology. Constant mutual surveillance "deeply rooted in daily life" stifles freedom of political expression and thinking (Kim et al. 2019 197).

2.3.2 Restrictive Social Policies and Surveillance

In addition to ideology and information control, North Korea's foundation of repression is built into its restrictive social policies and further reinforced by an elaborate system of surveillance. North Korea's hereditary-based and highly discriminatory *songbun* system sits at the center of this strategy. Established in the 1960s, this system stratifies North Koreans into one of three classifications – core, wavering, and hostile – which are then further subdivided into fifty-one categories (Collins 2012, 24).

Songbun determines every citizen's path of life to isolate and eliminate potential internal political threats. It dictates their access to employment, housing, education, health care, marriage, and even food rations. Those in the loyal core class, about 10 to 15 percent of the population, receive the best jobs, education, and housing (Fifield 2019, 121). Approximately 40 percent of the population falls into the bottom hostile class due to their tainted backgrounds (e.g. Japanese collaborators, capitalists, large landowners, pro-USA or pro-Japan sympathizers, and Christians) and resides in poor, rural areas. They are relegated to occupations involving hard labor or menial tasks with little opportunity for economic, social, or political advancement. The threat of being demoted to a lower *songbun*, or the greater scrutiny given to those in the wavering and hostile class, keeps elite and ordinary North Koreans from participating in antiregime activity. By rooting out suspected enemies of the state based on birth and family background, the *songbun* therefore serves as "the starting point for the regime's security policies . . . and enables the Kim regime to establish and reinforce its political control over all North Korean society" (Collins 2012, 1, 16).

Numerous restrictions against basic civil and political liberties such as the freedom of expression, freedom of thought and conscience, freedom of assembly, freedom of movement, and freedom of religion, among others, also strengthen the state's ideological control over society.[21] Expressing political thought contrary to revolutionary ideology, criticizing the Supreme Leader, and speaking positively about South Korea or the United States is to "misspeak" and can lead to imprisonment (Kim et al. 2019, 197). Domestic travel restrictions also prevent North Koreans from fomenting protests or widespread collective action. For example, short-term travel outside one's county or city requires authorization from local authorities. North Korean law stipulates that the People's Security Agency "shall exercise control over violations of travel regulations and disorderly wandering on the streets" (Kim et al. 2019, 16). To travel across different provinces, North Koreans must obtain a travel permit from the Office of the People's Committee. They must then report to the village head upon arrival at their destination, register their names on a travel roster, and obtain a Ministry of People's Security (MPS) stamped travel pass (Kim et al. 2019, 123–124).

The state uses its vast internal security system to surveil everyone from high-ranking party officials in Pyongyang to impoverished laborers in the provinces to ensure that everyone maintains their place in society and remains politically committed to the regime. An overlapping network of secret police and informants is used to prevent any institution from challenging the Supreme Leader. Thus, the lines of responsibility among intelligence and internal security forces are often blurred (Greitens 2016, 26). The key security institutions include the Ministry of State Security (MSS), the Ministry of People's Security (MPS), and the Military Security Command (MSC).

The MSS, known colloquially as the "*bowibu*" to North Koreans, operates as a secret police agency and is responsible for enforcing the regime's "monolithic

---

[21] Although Article 67 of North Korea's constitution states that citizens are granted the freedom of assembly and association, with the state guaranteeing "conditions for free activities of democratic parties and social organizations," in reality, the WPK and state-sponsored associations are the only organizations permitted (Kim et al. 2019, 220).

ideological system" (Person, n.d.). The MSS monitors antistate activities through surveillance, counterintelligence, and internal investigations (Collins and Oh 2017). The MSS also tracks political attitudes and conducts surveillance on North Koreans returning from overseas. Of the more than twenty bureaus which comprise the MSS, the most important units for maintaining internal regime security include bureau numbers 1 (general guidance), 2 (counterespionage), 4 (counterintelligence), 7 (prisons), 8 (border security), 10 (investigations), and 11 (prosecution) (Gause 2012, 19). More recently, Bureau 15, which oversees mobile communications, has played an important role with the rise of cell phones and attempts to make cross-border calls (Williams 2019, 15).

The MSS is complemented by the MPS or "*inmin boanbu*," which addresses nonpolitical crimes and carries out basic policing. As the national police, the MPS maintains law and order, investigates common criminal cases, monitors traffic, regulates travel, and administers the country's nonpolitical prison system (Gause 2012, 26). At the village level, MPS officers are more visible to North Koreans as they patrol the streets and maintain checkpoints to inspect buses, trucks, and trains, and ensure that travelers possess proper travel permits. The MPS also conducts unannounced home inspections including random spot checks between midnight to 3am to search for contraband or unapproved guests. The MSS and MPS in particular have deep surveillance networks throughout the country. For instance, Robert Collins (2019, 11) cites that the MPS maintains 4,000 office locations at the village or city subdistrict level with twenty to thirty personnel assigned to each office. The local offices "handle local criminal activity, check exit and entry of nonlocal residents, and maintain records on individual households" (Collins 2019, 11).

A crucial aspect of social control at the village level is the *inminban,* or neighborhood watch units. The *inminban* system is what enables the state to monitor each citizen at the level of households (Williams 2019, 13; Collins 2019, 12). Meetings are held twice a week and involve study sessions, lectures, and self-criticism that transmit political and ideological guidance to residents. With the exception of Kim Jong-un, all North Koreans, including party elites, are part of an *inminban* (Collins 2019, 42). The *inminban* is also used to mobilize residents for public works projects such as annual harvesting or village beautification campaigns.

The *inminban* is headed by an *inminbanjang* (neighborhood watch leader) who is recruited by the MSS.[22] The *inminbanjang*, typically a middle-aged woman in good standing with the party, works closely with the MSS and MPS to

---

[22] There are more recent reports, however, that some neighborhood watch leaders are being selected by residents themselves rather than local party leaders. See Kang 2018.

track suspicious behavior and conduct home inspections. The *inminbanjang* monitors a group of twenty to forty homes and reports any suspicious activity to authorities, especially possession of antiregime content found in DVDs, USBs, laptops, and other devices. Neighborhood informants are also embedded within watch units to report on activities that contradict the regime's ideology (Collins 2019, 45). Such tactics raise the level of suspicion and fear as neighbors and relatives are instructed to inform on one another and report on antirevolutionary behavior.

2.3.3 Violence and Coercion

Like most dictatorships, the North Korean regime uses fear, violence, and coercion to fend off elite challengers and suppress popular dissent. Public executions, political prisons, hard physical labor, and torture are routinely employed to deter individuals from participating in antiregime activity.

North Korea's penal system is particularly notorious for its inhumane treatment of political prisoners who are convicted without due process. Among the different types of prisons, North Koreans face the harshest treatment in the long-term penal labor colonies, or *kwanliso* (literally translated as control and management center). Political prisoners suspected of "wrong-doing, wrong-thinking, wrong-knowledge, wrong-association, or wrong-class-background" are sent to the *kwanliso* (Hawk 2012, 25). Their crimes include criticizing the regime, listening to foreign broadcasts, communicating with South Koreans, and attempting to defect abroad.

Former executive director of Amnesty International USA David Hawk (2012, 9) describes the *kwanliso* as "the incommunicado repositories for those North Korean citizens who have been cleansed or purged and deported to areas of North Korea outside the protection of the law." They are located in remote mountain valleys and consist of one or more villages, depending on the number of inmates, where prisoners are subjected to torture, hunger, malnutrition, poor sanitation, rape, forced abortions, and long hours of hard labor (Hassig and Oh 2015, 151). Due to North Korea's "guilt by association" (*yeonjwaje*), family members of guilty offenders have also been forcibly placed in prison, including entire families up to three generations.

In contrast to the *kwanliso*, which is reserved only for political criminals, convicted felons and common criminals are sent to the *kyohwaso*. Akin to penitentiaries or prisons, *kyohwaso* are translated euphemistically as "reeducation centers" (Hawk 2012, ix, 83; Hassig and Oh 2015, 149). Former prisoners describe the "education component" of imprisonment consisting of forced memorization of Kim Il-sung speeches and New Year's Day editorials, and organized self-criticism sessions. The education sessions are held in the evening after a full day of labor. Prisoners cannot return to their cells until they memorize speeches or confess to shirking duties if they miss their labor production quotas (Hawk 2012, 83). Although prison sentences are usually set for fixed terms, the combination of heavy labor and insufficient food rations results in high death rates (Hawk 2012, 83).

Political prisons serve an important function in the regime's system of social and political control. Not only do they punish and "rehabilitate" criminals, but they deter North Koreans from committing political crimes and isolate potential antirevolutionaries from infecting others with antiregime messages. For North Koreans considering defection, the possibility of sending family members to labor camps on account of one's defection has made some North Koreans think twice about escaping to China or South Korea. A number of defectors in South Korea have confessed to living with guilt knowing family members disappeared or were sent to prison after their defection, underscoring North Korea's use of intimidation and violence to prevent widespread dissent (Ryall 2019).

Like prisons, public executions send a stark reminder to anyone conspiring against the state.[23] Although cases of public executions have declined in recent years, a 2018 survey of defectors suggests that executions for drug trafficking and watching or distributing South Korean videos have increased (Kim et al. 2019, 15). Several North Korean defectors' testimonies have depicted students and workers mobilizing to attend public executions, particularly in border regions and in cities where illegal activities are more likely to occur (Kim et al. 2019, 64–66; UNCOI 2014, 262–68). A 2019 White Paper on Human Rights published by the Korea Institute for National Unification (KINU) in 2019 states that the regime uses public executions to "warn and incite fear among residents in those regions" (Kim et al. 2019, 66). Furthermore, the UNCOI (2014, 263) report on human rights in North Korea underscores the chilling effects of public executions, stating that "for young children and relatives of the victim, the experience of watching such killings is often so horrifying, that the witnesses must themselves also be considered victims of inhuman and cruel treatment."

2.3.4 Legitimating Strategies

Contrary to popular misconceptions that the regime remains static, the Kim dynasty adjusts to its changing internal and external environment. This might

---

[23] For an excellent discussion on the practice and performative aspects of public executions, see Fahy (2019, 149). Although North Korea's criminal code provides laws and regulations on capital punishment, there are no explicit guidelines on public executions.

entail a change in leadership personnel, or policy shifts in response to economic conditions or external security pressure. Beyond personnel and policy changes, however, authoritarian regimes rely on legitimating strategies, often through the use of ideology and propaganda, to address change and insulate leaders from criticism. The Kim regime is no exception: especially during hard times, the regime bolsters its legitimating strategies to minimize discontent and reframe its messaging to address hardships.

Alexander Dukalskis (2017, 60–61) helpfully unpacks these legitimating strategies into six components. *Concealment elements* "block, obscure, or euphemize undesirable aspects of the state's rules" with the intent of preventing public criticism and "unseemly aspects of rule from circulating in the public sphere." *Framing elements* "package particular events or issues so that they are consistent with the regime's ideology and legitimacy claims." *Inevitability elements* project a ruling class which is "unified, entrenched, and will rule in perpetuity." *Blaming elements* shift responsibility for negative outcomes onto other individuals, groups, or external states. *Mythologized origin elements* tie the current political leadership to the legitimacy of founding figures or to important events that trace a regime's lineage to historical origins. *Promised land elements* intend to "inspire hope about the future," and present "unfalsifiable evidence of regime 'success'" (Dukalskis 2017, 61).

Such strategies enable dictators to maintain some semblance of legitimacy, even in the wake of sharp "real world" contradictions that undercut the regime's ideology. For instance, during the 1990s, the regime's articulation of the famine as the "Arduous March" represented elements of framing and mythologized origin. The Arduous March was in direct reference to the hardships experienced by Kim Il-sung and his anti-Japanese guerilla fighters during the winter of 1938 and 1939, hence reminding North Koreans of the suffering experienced by their patriotic forefathers.[24] Likewise, during the transition to Kim Jong-un's rule in 2012, the regime relied on elements of inevitability and mythologized origin to shore up the young ruler's legitimacy. Kim Jong-un lacked experience, but his notable likeness in image to his grandfather, North Korea's founder, reminded citizens of the younger Kim's rightful destiny to rule. The regime also assigns blame for economic shortcomings and food shortages on US imperialism and a hostile policy of sanctions (KCNA 2016). Autocrats only need to keep the population at bay "most of the time" so long as they continue to minimize or marginalize challengers (Dukalskis 2017, 70).

---

[24] The regime adopted the slogan "Let Us All Become Victors in this Year's Arduous March" in 1997 (Dukalskis 2017, 76).

2.4 Conclusion

Despite the country's many shortcomings, the Kim family has reigned supreme in North Korea for three generations. To some, this may seem surprising. Why do North Koreans tolerate their leaders given the country's ongoing economic woes? For Pyongyang's elite, their fate may be tied to existing power structures. For ordinary North Koreans, fear, repression, ideological indoctrination, and information control may all work to prevent discontentment from boiling over.

The North Korean state wields immense power over society. Despite periodic signs of instability and predictions of regime collapse, Kim Jong-un solidified his rule within a few short years after ascending to power. Noting that "ideology and institutions [provide] the primary foundations for wielding power in modern Korea," and provided that they can be adapted to changing domestic and external circumstances, there is good reason to believe that the Kim family regime will continue to survive even beyond Kim Jong-un.

3 Rising Markets

> In the Democratic People's Republic of Korea, streets of distinctive features have been built every year, including Unha Scientists Street, Wisong Scientists Residential District and Mirae Scientists Street. This year Ryomyong Street, whose scale and amount of work were twice more than those of Mirae Scientists Street, was built in a short period of only one year. Ryomyong Street is a brilliant outcome of the country's independent national economy which is making rapid progress on the basis of its own strength, technology and resources under the banner of self-reliance and self-development, overcoming persistent and vicious economic sanctions and stifling schemes of the United States and its following forces.
>
> *–Foreign Trade*, April 2017 (Juche 106)

Ryomyong Street (see Figure 2) is one of several new luxury high-rise residential and commercial development projects in downtown Pyongyang, or "Pyonghattan" as described by Western visitors. Ryomyong opened with great fanfare in 2017 with thousands of spectators eagerly watching their beloved Supreme Leader cut the red ribbon (Fifield 2019, 145).

For a country associated more with mass famine and malnutrition than luxury condos and a pristine skyline, North Korea's economic situation has significantly improved since the 1990s. Journalists describe coffee shops, nail salons, massage parlors, and microbreweries springing up around Pyongyang. Two Western journalists in 2015 observed that "flaunting your wealth and consuming conspicuously is no longer frowned upon. From using a smartphone, flashing a Swiss watch, or carrying a designer bag, to drinking expensive coffee, what was once reserved for the upper elite is now a middle-class pastime"

Figure 2 High-rise buildings on Ryomyong Street in 2018. Photo courtesy of Andray Abrahamian.

(Tudor and Pearson 2015, 43). Commenting on changing women's fashion between 2005 and 2018, *Washington Post* correspondent Anna Fifield observed how young women in Pyongyang had traded conservative, communist tastes, "drab browns and grays and black, long skirts, shapeless jackets, functional shoes" for "more colorful and fitted clothes, sparkly jewelry, and look-at-me high heels" (Fifield 2019, 158). Just outside of Pyongyang, the *nouveau riche* can frolic in an amusement park, or enjoy a weekend ski trip near Wonsan.

Of course, these changes are limited to the capital and a few developed urban areas. Behind the facade of rapid development and economic growth, depicted neatly in North Korean propaganda outlets, cracks (literally) exist, underlining the poor state of the North Korean economy. Tiles were reportedly falling off new apartment buildings two years after their construction, and upper-floor units remain unoccupied (Fifield 2019, 146). Although the growth of the informal economy at the microlevel has generated tremendous wealth for some individual entrepreneurs and at the macrolevel has benefited the state coffers, North Korea's economy still remains one of the poorest in the world. North Korea's GDP[25] in real terms tracks below 1990 levels as indicated in Figure 3. And despite a large percentage of the workforce assigned to the agriculture sector,

---

[25] North Korea has not regularly published official economic statistics since the early 1980s. For an informative discussion on North Korean economic data and statistical biases, see Kim (2017, 72–83). Koen and Beom (2020, 7) also provide a list of sources on the North Korean economy.

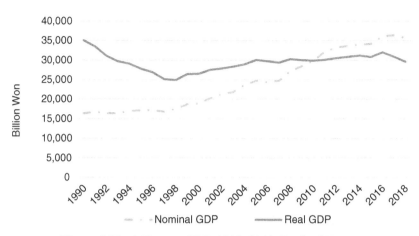

Figure 3 North Korean GDP, 1990–2018. Bank of Korea.

chronic malnourishment remains a problem (Koen and Beom 2020; United Nations DPRK Resident Coordinator 2019). Food shortages due to the COVID-19 pandemic and the ensuing border lockdown from January 2020 and well into 2021 have only exacerbated hunger and malnutrition.

Although North Korea has yet to transition to a market-based economy, the process of marketization carries potential long-term implications for both state and society. As Andrei Lankov (2013b) described, "North Korea nowadays is a country of booming black markets and an increasingly blurring line between state and private economies – essentially, a country of grassroots capitalism." Most North Koreans would not openly refer to themselves as capitalists – an identification that is a clear contradiction of North Korea's socialist revolution. After the Arduous March, however, the market economy has fostered an entrepreneurial spirit (Hastings 2016), turning many North Koreans into budding capitalists (Abrahamian 2020, 53). Marketization has taken place at multiple levels that differ in the degree of state involvement, the types of goods exchanged, and the scale of market activity. For instance, Sheena Greitens (2019, 130) has identified two distinct economic orders operating in parallel: "a Pyongyang-centered, elite-based order" relying on illicit transnational activity and state trading, and a bottom-up black or gray market operated by ordinary North Koreans near the Sino-North Korea border." Hastings et al. (2021, 10) have also described the structure of markets as multi-tiered: from local market traders at the very bottom, operating with minimal or no interaction with the state, to high-ranking party officials engaged in illicit trade in foreign markets at the very top. The regime has mostly tolerated market activity. However, it has sought to regulate and even periodically crack down on markets.

Over the past decade, Kim Jong-un has repeatedly stressed economic development as a national priority, whether as part of North Korea's dual track policy (or *byungjin*) of advancing the economy and nuclear weapons in tandem, or as an important end in its own right.[26] For instance, during his first five years of rule, Kim expanded the number of special economic zones throughout the country (Abrahamian 2014).[27] Yet as international sanctions, and later COVID-19 border lockdowns, tanked North Korea's economy, the regime tightened its control over markets. The rise of markets has thus been an uneven process. This section discusses the rise of markets in North Korea with a particular emphasis on the informal economy and the symbiotic relationships forged between state and market that both benefit and undermine the regime.

3.1 The Famine and the Rise of Markets

Like other planned central economies, the North Korean socialist economy experienced inefficiencies leading to a decline in economic performance from the 1960s. Faced with economic stagnation, North Korea experimented with market socialism in the 1980s – most notably through the August 3 People's Consumer Goods Production Movement (or the 8.3 movement), which addressed economic shortcomings by encouraging privatization (Gray and Lee 2021, 125). The 8.3 measures permitted workers to leave their official jobs and work in the informal sector for a certain number of days. In return, workers paid their state employers a fee (or bribe) with money earned through market activity.

Despite experiencing long-term economic decline, however, no major economic changes took place until the end of the Cold War. The loss of external support from the Soviet Union following its collapse and the onset of severe famine in the mid-1990s crippled North Korea's economy. Based on Bank of Korea (BOK) estimates, between 1990 and 1998, North Korea's per capita income plummeted by almost one-half from US$1,146 to US$573 (Kim 2017, 84).

The economic crisis also led to the collapse of the PDS, North Korea's system of allocating food rations.[28] Facing starvation, North Koreans resorted to foraging or grew their own food for private consumption. Surplus food, as

---

[26] See, for instance, the regime's five year economic plan unveiled during the WPK Congress in 2016 (Fifield 2016) and also Kim Jong-un's New Year's Day Speeches (available at NCNK 2019) – especially in 2019 when the term "economy" was mentioned thirty-nine times.

[27] In October 2013, the regime revealed plans for establishing thirteen new economic development zones at the provincial level (Abrahamian 2014, 14).

[28] For a useful discussion of the PDS and its breakdown, see Haggard and Noland 2007, 58–62; Robinson 2019.

well as consumer goods, were bartered or sold in makeshift markets (Kim 2017, 47; Smith 2015, 203). Small-scale farmers' markets eventually developed into larger-scale black markets after the famine in a process of marketization from below or what Hazel Smith (2015, 213) calls "marketization by default."

Over time, marketization evolved from a "bottom-up survival process" to one "partly managed at the top" as the regime tolerated but also sought to wrest control over markets (Koen and Beom 2020, 33). By the early 2000s, two policy measures in particular indicated the regime's acceptance of markets on a limited basis. The first was the regime's implementation of the "July 1 Measures" (or 7.1 measures) in 2002, which decentralized economic planning at the local level. The 7.1 measures granted SOEs greater autonomy in setting production targets and prices, and the ability to buy and sell capital inputs and other goods through markets (Kim 2017, 51; Kim and Yang 2015, 18). Unable to rely only on Pyongyang for resources, regional governments looked to markets and private investors to obtain inputs, consumer goods, and food. By decentralizing economic authority down to the production-unit level and granting SOEs flexibility to finance their own business, state bureaucrats turned to markets to procure resources and sell finished products (Lankov 2013a, 120). As Byrne and Corrado (2019, 10–11) posit, "What followed was an ongoing, countrywide negotiation for economic autonomy between state and society in North Korea, as rigidly centralized political institutions condoned gradual decentralization in exchange for a cut of the profits."

Second, the regime legalized hundreds of black markets in March 2003. Until then, markets had been operating without any legal status since the famine.[29] Farmers' markets selling a wide variety of goods beyond food and basic necessities were referenced as *jonghap sijang* or "general markets" (Lankov 2013a, 120; Gray and Lee 2021, 146). In the short run, the legalization of markets had little real impact on the everyday behavior of market participants who continued business as usual, except for the requirement of paying vendor stall fees and additional "tax" to the state. Informal, unregulated markets continued to coexist with these "regularized, state-sponsored markets" (Collins 2018, 5).

The July 1 measures, as well as the legalization of farmers' markets, were seen as reactive in that the regime had "little choice but to accept and legitimize the expanded role of the market" (Gray and Lee 2021, 144). However, they were

---

[29] There is some discrepancy on whether general markets were legalized following the approval of the 7.1 measures in 2002 (see Lankov 2013a, 120), or later in 2003 through "cabinet decision No. 27 and cabinet guideline No. 24" (Lee 2019a). Regardless, the formalization of general markets may best be interpreted as part of an ongoing process of marketization following the 7.1 measures.

proactive in the sense that the regime had gradually shifted away from a centrally planned economy to one which increasingly utilized market mechanisms. The July 1 measures were initially heralded by the outside world as a sign of North Korea embracing economic reforms. In hindsight, the measures were more likely implemented to stabilize the socialist economy rather than transition to a market economy (Kim 2017, 65).

3.2 Private Entrepreneurs and SOEs

The role of private entrepreneurs, or *donju* (translated as "masters of money" or "wealthy private financiers"),[30] and their relationship to the state expanded with marketization. Whereas the early days of markets mostly entailed private individuals buying and selling food and basic commodities to earn a living, by the late 2000s, markets had evolved to include service providers, wholesale and retail sellers, brokers, and private investors working with SOEs to amass profit (Byrne and Corrado 2019, 10). Private investment in SOEs "became widespread in restaurants and shops, and thereafter, spread to trading companies, factories, cooperative farms, fisheries, mining, and construction enterprises" (Gray and Lee 2021, 155). SOEs and other state institutions became major beneficiaries and also key actors in markets.[31] In addition to offering the *donju* "legal" operating status in return for private financing, SOEs distributed finished goods through markets and used their profit to pay state-salaried workers (Daily NK 2017, 41).

Beyond the general market for consumer goods, four other market sectors have emerged in the areas of service, real estate, finance, and labor (NK Daily 2017). The service sector has seen the most growth and greatest activity in the informal economy since the 2010s. Service-related jobs have emerged in wholesale and retail sales, food services, personal services (e.g. hair care, shoe repair), childcare, and delivery and transportation (Kim and Yang 2015, 26–27; Daily NK 2017, 44–45).

---

[30] *Donju* have accumulated wealth through a variety of means. *Donju* include individuals with access to foreign currency and networks, such as Chinese residents in North Korea (*hwagyo*), ethnic Koreans, Chinese nationals (*chonsonjok*), and long-time Korean residents in Japan. *Donju* are also connected to the state and can include SOE managers or a relative or spouse of party officials. Some *donju* previously worked in trading companies under the WPK, the military, and government agencies. By working in positions related to foreign trade, and with access to finance, the *donju* "expanded their economic activities in markets, including for consumer goods, transport, distribution, and money lending" (Koen and Beom 2020, 32).

[31] Note that SOEs still belong to the formal economy, even if they rely on markets for transactions. However, private entrepreneurs may exploit, bribe, or use assets from SOEs for their private gain. The latter actions are considered part of the informal economy. As Kim and Yang (2015, 13) clarify, the informal economy focuses on private ownership and economic agents and exists outside of formal legal and administrative frameworks. Parts of the formal economy may rely on market mechanisms to allocate resources, but such activities may still be considered a part of the formal economy. See Figure 5.

As an example of the latter, marketization created a new demand for delivery, ground transportation, and logistics operations resulting in the development of "*servi-cha*" vehicles (Y. Kim 2019). Vehicles registered to state institutions such as the military and SOEs were "rented" to transport goods, money, and people in exchange for a fee. In the 1990s, vehicles available for transportation and shipping were limited to freight and military trucks. With marketization, the variety of *servi-cha* vehicles expanded to include buses, vans, motorcycles, and taxis to address short and long distance delivery and travel needs (Y. Kim 2019). Local and interregional bus networks connecting major cities were also developed with market activity bustling along bus stop lines (NK Daily 2017, 47; interviewee #16,[32] interview by the author, June 6, 2019).

Reflecting the symbiotic relationship between state and markets, the regime permits vehicle "owners" to operate a *servi-cha* in return for vehicle registration fees and a percentage of profits. As ownership of private property is still prohibited, *servi-cha* are technically registered and owned by the state. Once registered, however, a vehicle "owner" can transport people or goods, either directly or by hiring other drivers, to make deliveries between China and North Korea or within North Korea (Gray and Lee 2021, 157).

In addition to transportation and delivery services, an informal housing market and real estate boom emerged in the mid-2010s in Pyongyang. The regime supposedly offers housing to all citizens – as reaffirmed in North Korea's 2009 Housing Law. In theory then, private home ownership and an official real estate market should not exist in North Korea (NK Daily 2017, 62). Nevertheless, the *donju* provide SOEs with capital, finance, and materials to build high-rise apartments and commercial buildings in a de facto public-private joint venture. In return, SOEs remunerate the *donju* by granting them building usage rights which offer a higher return than initial investments (Koen and Beom 2020, 32; Lee 2019b). Individuals then sell (or buy) government-issued housing usage permits. The exchange of housing usage rights has generated a "hybrid form" of informal property rights with tacit support from the state (Gray and Lee 2021, 163). Real estate prices have increased significantly in newly developed sections of Pyongyang where five-room apartments in the Central District sold for US$200,000 in 2017 (Gray and Lee 2021, 163).[33]

In short, private entrepreneurs have taken advantage of market gray areas to earn money and establish businesses under the guise of (or in partnership with) SOEs. Retail and food distribution networks initially established by the state are

---

[32] All interviews were conducted in confidentiality, and the names of interviewees are withheld by mutual agreement.

[33] Housing prices may have since dropped with prolonged sanctions and COVID-19 restrictions reducing the money supply.

now run by entrepreneurs through the private market, even if they nominally operate within the purview of the state (NK Daily 2017, 51). Lankov et al. (2017, 51) have referred to these SOEs as "pseudo-state enterprises" that are "state-run and owned on paper, but in practice controlled by private interests to which much of the profits accrued." Underscoring the mutually self-reinforcing relationship between state and market, SOEs receive "de facto quasi-tax contributions from individuals" in exchange for operating rights (Koen and Beom 2020, 32). The *donju*, WPK officials, and state bureaucrats alike have amassed significant wealth. A few SOEs have even evolved into something akin to Korean *chaebol* (family-owned business conglomerates). For instance, North Korea's state-owned airline, Air Koryo, runs multiple businesses including gas stations, taxis, soft drinks, and cigarettes (Wong and Pearson 2017).

3.3 The Size and Significance of Markets

Although the exact size and scope of markets in North Korea is unknown, several defector surveys, corroborated by satellite and geospatial imagery, suggest that their role in daily life has expanded greatly during the past two decades (Haggard and Noland 2007, 2017; Lankov et al. 2017; Kim and Yang 2015; IPUS 2020). In fact, markets have become the primary source of income for most households. Researchers in a Daily NK study from 2017 reported 387 officially sanctioned markets across the country with an estimated 4 million North Koreans making their earnings through market activities (Daily NK 2017, 26). In a country with roughly 25 million people, the existence of 612,661 general market stalls suggests one stall per forty North Koreans. Some of the largest markets such as the Toksan Farmers' Market in South Pyongan Province include over 8,000 market stalls (NK Daily 2017, 26). Researchers at the Beyond Parallel project at the Center for Strategic and International Studies (CSIS) confirmed at least 436 officially sanctioned markets (see Figure 4) in 2018 (Cha and Collins 2018), and economist Curtis Melvin recorded 480 markets the same year (RFA 2018).

The prevalence of markets in North Korea is also found in several defector surveys. Economist Byung-yeon Kim's (2017, 100) survey of defectors revealed that more North Koreans participated in the informal economy (71.2 percent) than the official economy (50.6 percent).[34] Kim (2017, 103) also found that North Koreans' average monthly income from the informal economy was eighty times higher than income generated from their state-sanctioned jobs. North Koreans spent more hours in their informal jobs with

---

[34] All defector surveys carry inherent biases and issues with reliability, but Kim's survey of recent defectors (at the time of sampling) appear to better control for geography, income level, and hindsight bias. See Kim 2017, 94–97.

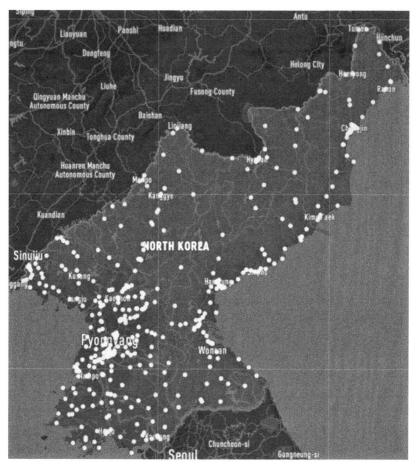

Figure 4 Location of official markets in North Korea in 2018. In Cha and Collins 2018. © 2018 by Beyond Parallel and CSIS, in partnership with North Korea Development Institute.

the main forms of work found in cultivating garden plots, cattle feeding, trading, smuggling, and repairing consumer goods. The primary reason (61.6 percent) for North Koreans working in the informal sector was attributed to insufficient income from their formal sector job (Kim 2017, 104). General markets, which the state approved in 2003, are today the largest provider of consumer goods in North Korea (Daily NK 2017, 30).

Kim's survey findings also indicate that North Koreans relied heavily on markets to obtain food, with 60 percent of defectors stating that they relied on markets compared to 22.6 percent who used official channels (state-supplied rations and state retail shops). Likewise, 68.7 percent of defectors surveyed stated that they purchased consumer goods through markets compared with

17.8 percent of defectors receiving goods from state channels (Kim 2017, 118). A series of surveys conducted by IPUS from 2012 to 2019 support these numbers, indicating around 70 percent of households participating in informal markets (IPUS 2020, 33). As reported by Daily NK (2017, 40), "The market system provides a degree of comfort that was unimaginable under the PDS of the Kim Il-sung era."

3.4 State Intervention and Markets

Scholars fundamentally agree that private-market actors and the state have developed a mutually beneficial relationship.[35] However some debate exists regarding the degree to which markets have expanded "by default" (Smith 2015, 212) as opposed to the state playing a more leading role in the process of marketization (Gray and Lee 2021, 28). Between the period of the Arduous March and the July 1, 2002 measures, market dynamics were more likely to be spontaneous with the regime reacting to conditions on the ground rather than leading any reforms (Haggard and Noland 2017, 48). As market mechanisms expanded, however, the regime played a more assertive role in intervening in markets from the mid-2000s. In 2005, the regime attempted to revive the PDS and reassert its authority over the food market by declaring a ban on private trade in grain; however, the PDS lacked sufficient resources to meet daily rations, and North Koreans continued to depend on markets. Seeking to redirect market income from private actors, in 2006 the regime launched a bond sale but failed to generate significant revenue (Byrne and Corrado 2019, 10). In 2007, the regime prohibited women under the age of forty (or fifty depending on the region) – the primary demographic of market vendors – from working in markets. In 2008, the regime declared markets would only operate three days a week (Hassig and Oh 2015, 47–48).

None of the above measures succeeded in reining in markets. On November 30, 2009, in a much more draconian effort to roll back markets and address the widening gap between official and market prices, the regime redenominated the value of the North Korean won at a ratio of one hundred to one (i.e. one hundred old won was revalued at one new won). North Koreans were initially given just seven days to trade their old bills for the new currency with a maximum limit of 100,000 won (or about US$30). Shortly thereafter, the regime banned the use of foreign currency. Traders who hoarded hard-earned

---

[35] As Byung-yeon Kim (2017, 159) writes, "the informal economy is interconnected with the official economy in terms of the labor input and output markets." Bribery and corruption also exist at the intersection of the formal and informal economy and have become an important, if not necessary, element of North Korean marketization.

cash in the markets were hit hardest as they saw their savings disappear overnight. In contrast, workers dependent on the formal economy were "rewarded" as their salaries increased one-hundred fold (Lankov 2013a, 127).

The regime's attempt to weaken market mechanisms through currency reform backfired. Mass confusion and strong backlash pushed the regime to raise the limit of currency exchanges to 150,000 won in cash, and 300,000 won in deposits (Koen and Beom 2020, 13). Within six months, the regime was forced to reopen previously banned markets and allow the circulation of foreign currency (Haggard and Noland 2017, 49). The top official in charge of the currency reform was reportedly executed. Whereas markets continued to flourish, faith in the formal economy eroded further as North Koreans clung to Chinese yuan, and to a lesser extent US dollars, to hedge against the depreciating North Korean won (Lee 2018, 54; Hastings 2016, 100–101).

Ultimately, markets have prevailed, even as the regime periodically tightens market restrictions. However, the underlying tension between state and market forces remains unsettled since markets exist at the intersection of the formal and informal economy (see Figure 5). Certain segments of the market that trade in high value or high volume goods procured through SOEs will continue to experience state involvement in contrast to those markets operating at the grassroots or outside the purview of the state (interviewee #24, interview by the author, May 15, 2020).

Here, the scale and scope of market activity matters. Small entrepreneurs conducting business using local currency in the general markets tend to operate with minimal intervention from the state. Their interaction with the state may amount to paying small bribes or fees for conducting business (Hastings et al. 2021; Lee 2019a). Individuals trading higher value commodities in foreign

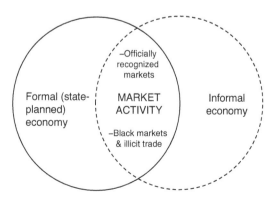

Figure 5 Markets at the intersection of the formal and informal economies. Adapted from Cha and Collins 2018.

currency will require state-issued trading licenses and/or access to party or military elites. *Donju* investing in joint public-private ventures will likely need to register their business under an SOE. At the top, party officials and SOE managers will be heavily vested in market activities, leasing out trading rights and other resources in the market (Hastings 2016, 113–17).

Additionally, the level of state control and intervention in markets will vary by region (Greitens 2019, 132). In Pyongyang, party elites engage in illicit trade networks involving weapons, drugs, and narcotics. In contrast, the economic activity of ordinary North Koreans residing along the Sino-North Korea border, especially in North Hamgyong province, will revolve around small, informal markets involving goods smuggled from China. The role of states in markets and conversely the relative freedom and leverage market actors exercise over states will depend on the size, location, and scope of market activity in North Korea.

3.5 Sanctions, Pandemics, and Markets

Despite the relatively permissive market environment developed during the Kim Jong-un era, international sanctions linked to nuclear proliferation have dealt a serious blow to Chairman Kim's longer term economic vision. The real impact of sanctions on North Korean markets is not entirely clear, although it is reasonable to assume that markets would be faring much better were sanctions to be lifted.

On the one hand, a decline in trade of sanctioned goods such as oil, iron, and coal suggests slower economic growth since 2017.[36] Imports from China in 2018 decreased by 88 percent from the previous year. Such a sharp decrease would surely have affected markets, even with ongoing illicit trade across the Sino-Korea border (Choe 2019). A report produced by Korea Peace Now (2019) also outlined the significant impact of sanctions on the humanitarian needs and development capacity of North Koreans. UN sanctions have banned trade in minerals, placed caps on imported oil and gas, prohibited the export of textiles and seafood, and prevented new North Korean workers from overseas employment (Korea Peace Now 2019, 16–17). An anecdote reflecting the effect of sanctions on markets in both the informal and formal sectors suggests that *donju* in Musan – a city known for iron-ore production – went bankrupt. Meanwhile, miners working in the formal sector lost their jobs in the absence of iron exports (Choe 2019). The loss of Chinese investment due to sanctions

---

[36] See BOK estimates for 2018 and 2019, which indicate a decline in economic growth since 2017 (*Gross Domestic Product Estimates for North Korea in 2018*, Press Release [Bank of Korea, July 26, 2019], www.bok.or.kr/eng/bbs/E0000634/view.do?nttId=10053001&menuNo=400069).

has also undermined Kim Jong-un's efforts to develop new SEZs throughout North Korea aimed at tourism and technology. Experts predicted that the regime would lose a minimum of US$1 billion per year in foreign reserves without sanctions relief – an untenable situation in the long run (Kim 2019).

On the other hand, North Korea has actively circumvented sanctions (UNSC 2020). Reports of infrastructure projects such as renewed bridge construction connecting Dandong in China to Sinuiju in North Korea, and pavement for a new bridge linking the North Korean border city of Namyang to Tumen, China in 2019, also indicate ongoing infrastructure development despite heavy sanctions (O'Carroll and Brehm 2018, 9). Stable exchange rates and the price of rice (at least up through 2020) suggest the limited effect of sanctions in local markets (Koen and Beom 2020, 13, 15; Daily NK 2018; Silberstein 2020a). As usual, North Koreans have managed to muddle through despite adversity, in no small part due to illicit trade activities (UNSC 2020).

The COVID-19 pandemic in early 2020 marked a much more significant blow to North Korea's economy than sanctions, given the extreme quarantine measures and border lockdown enacted by the regime to prevent the spread of the coronavirus (Choe 2020a). As economist Bradley Babson (2020) argues, "The short-term economic shock from the closure of the border with China for both trade and tourism has accomplished in a matter of weeks what United Nations Security Council sanctions have failed to achieve since their expansion in 2017 to commercial sectors." In particular, the complete closure of the Sino-North Korea border during the first half of 2020, and restrictions on cross-border flows of people and goods, have crippled market traders. In addition to shutting down borders and disrupting smuggling networks, the regime restricted domestic travel and commerce and set price controls on goods sold at markets (Wertz 2020).

Trade with China during the first half of 2020 declined by 67 percent compared with the same period in 2019 (Choe 2020b). At the height of North Korea's lockdown in March and April 2020, Sino-North Korea trade decreased by up to 93 percent (Yonhap News 2020). To make matters worse, severe summer flooding exacerbated conditions with the Supreme Leader admitting that economic shortcomings had been caused by "unexpected and inevitable challenges in various aspects" (Associated Press 2020). Yet as reported in North Korea's *Rodong Sinmun* (2020a), the regime continued to prioritize coronavirus pandemic measures over economic projects, declaring that borders would remain closed until the arrival of a vaccine.

Paradoxically, even though market dynamics have grown in importance under Kim Jong-un, the regime may decide to tighten control over private markets as sanctions and strict pandemic quarantine measures weigh down on the economy

(Silberstein 2020a). Signs of increasing state intervention have been visible since 2018 as the regime has asserted greater authority over foreign trade, increased market vendor stall fees, and discouraged the use of foreign currency (Wertz 2020).

At the fifth plenary meeting of the Seventh Central Committee of WPK in December 2019, Kim Jong-un stated that the regime should "strengthen the state's finances by making effective use of the existing economic foundations, and undertake economic planning properly, and scrupulously command the economic activities" (NCNK 2020). In his speech, Kim also criticized the state's economic planners for failing to spur "self-reliance and self-development" and the need for the cabinet to "rationally organize" the economic system and strengthen "the state's unified guidance over management of the economic work." Chairman Kim also chastised officials for engaging in bribery and corruption, for which he seized the assets of dozens of *donju* (Jeong and Martin 2019). The extreme measures of control the state has undertaken during the pandemic may encourage the regime to continue asserting its authority over local market actors (Wertz 2020).

In early 2021, several signs are indeed pointing to tighter control over markets in the wake of yet another economic crisis. This includes statements from party officials calling for greater economic control; reported restrictions on the use of foreign currency; reports of new policies reversing decentralizing trends and placing the management of general markets under direct state control; and amending enterprise laws to place private enterprise under state scrutiny (Silberstein 2020a). Dwindling resources and cash reserves in the midst of sanctions and the pandemic may explain the regime's renewed efforts to rein in private markets and corruption (Silberstein 2020b). However, the regime also recognizes the more fundamental problem of the market's role in undermining its authority and legitimacy. A KCNA report summarizing a November 30, 2020 politburo meeting stated that the Party Central Committee sought to strengthen its ideological outreach and "improve party guidance" over economic work. This was followed by Kim Jung-un's call for greater economic centralization at the Eighth Congress of the Korean Workers' Party in January 2021 (Frank 2021).

3.6 Conclusion

The role of markets and their place within the formal, state-controlled economy will continue to evolve and move in fits and starts. For instance, the regime recognizes "the existence of certain markets and related practices" (NK Daily 2017, 25), but also regulates markets by levying a tax on earnings and requiring sellers to pay market stall fees (Hassig and Oh 2015, 47; Yang 2020). The regime periodically attempts to exert control over markets, but each time, market forces have prevailed (Hastings 2016, 98). This is consistent with the push-and-pull dynamics and nonlinear trajectory of market reforms pursued in other communist countries such as China.

Positive feedback loops linking the state and markets make it nearly impossible for the state to shut down markets completely. As Justin Hastings (2016, 98) observes, "Both state and non-state actors have to interact with each other and, just as importantly, become more like each other in this new environment in which their activities are technically illegal but unstoppable on a large scale because the state depends on activity it has banned for its survival." Hence, North Korea "has evolved into a society with markets in everything" (Hastings 2016, 173). The participation of state officials in market activity also legitimates and normalizes the role of markets in daily North Korean life (Smith 2015, 220). This holds true even as the regime adjusts to the effects of sanctions and the COVID-19 pandemic by cracking down on corruption and reasserting greater control over markets. However, past regime attempts to rein in markets have not been successful, and the Kim family may face a crisis of legitimacy if markets (both official and unofficial) continue to remain outside of official state ideology and discourse.

4 State, Society, and the Question of Legitimacy

These unofficial, sometimes "hidden" practices point emphatically to the gap between compliance and belief. They help to establish an Aesopian public sphere, an alternative space in which official rhetoric and imagery are invoked only to be criticized, undermined, transgressed, or subverted.

–Lisa Wedeen (2015, 130).

Since the Arduous March, North Koreans have become increasingly dependent on the market economy. However, the impact of markets on state-society relations is less clear. One thesis is that markets continue to reflect and sustain state power. Low-level market participants operating in the general and black markets must operate within the boundaries of state authority where the regime extracts "rent" from market vendors. Wealthier *donju* colluding with party officials help fill state coffers, yet are still subject to state control as evidenced in vulnerability to crackdowns against corruption (Jong 2020; Ward 2020). At the top, party officials run illicit trade networks that help keep the selectorate (i.e. the narrow band of ruling elites surrounding the regime) satisfied with material benefits such as luxury goods – thereby ensuring regime stability.

The antithesis is that market forces diffuse power from the state to market actors, who in turn gradually empower society as markets help establish informal trust networks, hollow out the formal economy, and undermine state control. North Koreans shirk duties in their official workplace to take on informal sector jobs (Joo 2010, 132–33). Entrepreneurs frequently bribe officials to facilitate transactions (Kim 2017). North Koreans acquire knowledge about the outside world through markets and foreign outlets rather than through official state channels (Kretchun et al. 2017). All these activities precipitated by markets work to erode the ideological foundation of the regime. Markets thus challenge the limits of authoritarian rule as ordinary North Koreans and party elites behave in ways that deviate from the regime's official ideology.

Juxtaposed to these two perspectives, this section examines how market forces have shaped state-society relations in two ways in a direction more conducive to societal development. First, markets have created a gap between public and private (hidden) transcripts (i.e. the words spoken and actions taken by North Koreans in their everday life), allowing space for a semipublic sphere to operate. Second, markets have shifted the direction and content of information flow with the rise of informal trust networks. The state still remains a powerful stakeholder and regulator of markets, but it also depends on and reacts to private actor movement. This suggests a feedback mechanism that allows information to move from society to state, and not just from state to society. More importantly, information, including content from outside of North Korea, appears to be flowing horizontally among personal and/or market-based informal trust networks.

The first part of this section presents evidence from defector surveys and field-worker interviews that suggests both elements of change and continuity in state-society relations with the rise of markets. The second part then context-ualizes the data within existing comparative and theoretical frameworks for understanding state-society relations and evaluates whether everyday resistance and market-based, semi-public information networks have given society rela-tively greater autonomy and power vis-à-vis the state.

4.1 Empirical Insights on North Korean Societal Attitudes

4.1.1 IPUS Surveys on Unification Perceptions and Social Change

Methodological issues notwithstanding,[37] several defector surveys have shed light on North Korea and improved our understanding of the circumstances, conditions, and challenges confronting the defector population prior to and after defection. This section relies on surveys published by IPUS at Seoul National University for two reasons. First, the IPUS surveys on North Korean unification perceptions and social change[38] have been conducted yearly since 2008[39] and therefore offer

---

[37] See Section 1.5 for a discussion on methodological problems related to defector surveys and interviews.

[38] Surveys are published in two comprehensive reports available at https://ipus.snu.ac.kr/blog/archives/research_cat/unification_perception-survey and https://ipus.snu.ac.kr/blog/archives/research_cat/nksurvey.

[39] The exception is 2010, when a new sampling methodology was implemented.

systematic data on North Korean defectors over time. The number of respondents per year ranges from a high of 370 to a low of 87 with an average of 163. To increase data reliability, from 2011, the sample only included individuals who had defected from North Korea within the previous twelve months (e.g. respondents surveyed in 2019 all left North Korea no later than 2018). Second, the surveys include several questions related to North Korean leadership, ideology, and social change, thus providing greater insight on the degree of stability and change in North Korea.

Consistent with other studies involving defector surveys and interviews (Kim 2017; Choi 2013; Haggard and Noland 2007), the IPUS surveys indicate that the majority of defectors (on average 70 percent) have participated in market activity, as shown in Figure 6. Despite widespread exposure to markets, responses from defector surveys do not seem to suggest any obvious collective challenge to the regime or its ideology.

For instance, when asked in 2019 what percentage of the North Korean population they believed still supported Chairman Kim, 71.6 percent of survey respondents believed that at least half of all North Koreans still supported their leader. Support for Kim Jong-un slightly increased from 2018 to 2019, and remained higher than support for Kim Jong-il during the elder Kim's last three years of rule, as shown in Figure 7.[40]

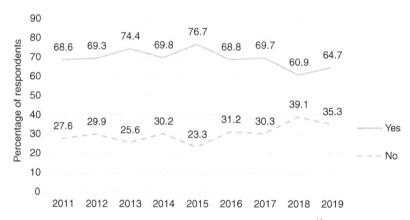

Figure 6 Experience with business activity in North Korea.[41] IPUS 2020, 33.

---

[40] The IPUS surveys reveal slight variation across regions and age cohorts, with defectors in North Hamgyong province and younger North Koreans indicating less support for the regime. This supports existing arguments that the post-famine *jangmadang* generation and North Koreans living in border regions with access to outside information are more likely to express criticism towards the regime (Park 2018; Baek 2016).

[41] The wording of the question was "When living in North Korea, did you have any experience with business?" (귀하는 북한에 살고 계실 때 장사를 한 경험이 있습니까?) (IPUS 2020, 278). The question was phrased as "business experience" since defectors may have been unfamiliar with the phrase "market participation."

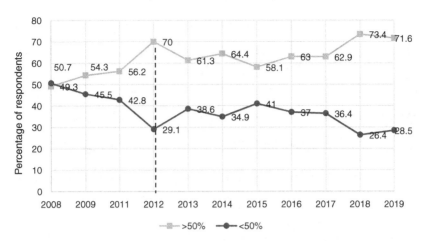

Figure 7 Approval rating of Kim Jong-il and Kim Jong-un (indicated by the percentage of defectors who believed Kim's approval rating was above or below 50 percent). IPUS 2020, 109.[42]

Interestingly, defectors indicated that a majority of North Koreans approved of Kim Jong-un as a leader, even though more than half of defectors in 2019 (and in previous years) judged his performance as head of state as less than satisfactory. In 2019, 55 percent of defectors had a negative perception of Kim's performance (which 29 percent judged as poor and 25 percent as very poor), while 44 percent of defectors had a positive impression of Kim's performance (36 percent believed Kim was performing very well and 8 percent believed he was performing well). In other words, perceptions of Kim Jong-un's approval rating were not necessarily tied to perceptions of his performance as a leader.

As with limited support for Kim Jong-un, Figure 8 reveals that the majority of North Korean defectors surveyed between 2008 and 2019 indicated that they took some level of pride in *juche* ideology, despite expressing greater ambivalence between the years 2013 and 2016. In 2019, 61.2 percent of defectors expressed a sense of pride in *juche* (34.5 percent stated that they felt a great sense of pride and 26.7 percent some sense of pride), in contrast to 38.8 percent of respondents who did not (29.3 percent took little pride and 9.5 percent no pride in *juche*). One explanation for increased pride in *juche* since 2016 may relate to the rise in militaristic rhetoric associated with missile and nuclear

---

[42] The exact wording of the question was "When living in North Korea, what was the level of support for Chairman Kim Jong-un?" (귀하는 북한에 살고 계실 때 김정은 국무위원장에 대한 북한주민들의 지지도가 어느 정도라고 생각하셨습니까?). Note that not all responses add up to 100 percent due to survey nonresponses.

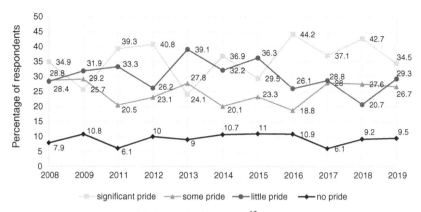

Figure 8 Pride in *juche* ideology.[43] IPUS 2020, 106.

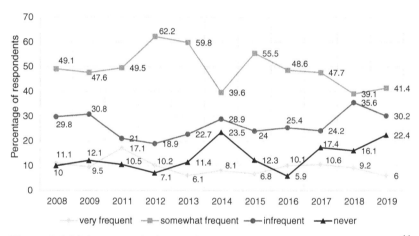

Figure 9 Criticism towards the North Korean government. IPUS 2020, 113.[44]

achievements in 2016 and 2017, followed by high profile summits between North Korea and the United States in 2018 and 2019.[45]

As with increased pride in *juche* and support for the regime, when defectors were asked whether they witnessed outward acts of criticism or

---

[43] Note that not all responses add up to 100 percent due to survey nonresponses.

[44] The exact wording of the question is "When living in North Korea, how much criticism/acts of criticism (graffiti, leaflets) towards the leader or government did you think existed? (귀하는 북한에 살고 계실 때 북한에 지도자나 정부에 대한 비판 행위(낙서, 삐라 등)가 얼마나 있다고 생각하셨습니까?). Since the question referred to specific actions, I translated responses as referring to the frequency of incidents, even though the literal translation is recorded as "a lot" or "a little."

[45] Support for *juche* may also remain high if North Koreans equate *juche* with North Korean nationalism. It is unclear to what extent "pride in *juche*" reflects the socialist aspect of the regime's ideology, which reportedly few North Koreans buy into in the era of markets, as opposed to the nationalist dimension of *juche* ideology.

resistance against the North Korean government when living in North Korea such as graffiti or distribution of antigovernment propaganda, defectors indicated a gradual decrease in such acts of criticism as shown in Figure 9. In the most recent 2019 survey, 53 percent of defectors stated that they observed little or no form of criticism when living in North Korea, whereas 47 percent stated that they witnessed some forms of criticism against the regime.

Of course, decreasing criticism may also be interpreted as a sign of the regime tightening its grip over society. However, the fact that almost half of North Koreans perceived *any* acts of outward criticism towards the regime is telling. Moreover, when defectors were asked to what degree public security agencies maintained social control over the population in 2019, 68.9 percent of respondents stated that social control was not being maintained well or at all. This was more than twice the number of defectors (31.1 percent) who stated that social control was being maintained well or only somewhat well (IPUS 2020, 275). In fact, between 2011 and 2019, the majority of defectors thought the regime was unable to maintain a firm grip over society.

In sum, based on IPUS defector surveys from 2008 and 2019, support for Kim Jong-un and a sense of his legitimacy generally seems strong, even though acts of criticism, dissent, and disobedience (at least among North Koreans near the border areas) are relatively common occurrences. These findings corroborate other studies that note the duality of everyday life in North Korea and other highly authoritarian places where citizens reproduce the regime's "formulaic slogans" and remain outwardly obedient, but privately question, criticize, or defy the regime's directives (Dukalskis and Joo 2020; Baek 2016; Choi 2013; Wedeen 2015; Kuran 1991).[46] Nowhere is this duality more present than in the market sphere where the very act of market participation (i.e. capitalism) *should* violate the regime's core revolutionary (i.e. socialist) principles.

Although market participation, especially in the informal economy, may be construed as a disobedient act (even if party officials also engage in and enable such "disobedience"), one cannot infer from defector surveys that a high level of market participation weakens state control. I therefore draw on additional insights from interviews and discussions held with North Korean field-workers and experts, as well as the secondary literature on North Korean markets and society, to offer greater nuance and context.

---

[46] This does not imply that North Koreans are necessarily disloyal or see their rulers as illegitimate. Whereas some North Koreans may be fed up with the regime, others may compartmentalize positive and negative aspects of the regime and its ideology.

4.1.2 Additional Field-Worker Insights

Between 2014 and 2020, I conducted twenty-seven interviews with foreign (i.e. non-North Korean) field-workers and experts.[47] Of this group, seventeen individuals had resided in or regularly travelled to North Korea for business (five), humanitarian and/or development work (eight), and/or academic, scientific, and cultural exchanges (four).[48] I have also participated in dozens of private or off-the-record discussions, either individually or in a group setting, with NGO workers, academic researchers, and policy experts who work closely with defectors or have regular access to contacts in North Korea and are knowledgeable about market dynamics and North Korean society. Since most interviews and roundtable discussions were not-for-attribution or off-the-record, and to protect the identities of field-workers given the sensitive nature of their work, their collective insights are shared as part of a broader discussion about social and political life in North Korea – unless they granted permission to share specific observations. I have also drawn from my own (admittedly limited) interactions with North Korean defectors over the past decade to supplement information from defector surveys and field-worker insights.

Although North Koreans may recognize economic shortcomings – as with any nation – many remain proud of their country. When I met in 2013 and again in 2014 a delegation of about a dozen college students who had defected from North Korea and were visiting Washington, DC (under the sponsorship of an NGO), the majority of students told me that they hoped to find a career or vocation that would allow them to help other North Koreans, or help support the process of Korean unification.[49] In other words, North Koreans still cared deeply about their home country and its future. A field-worker who regularly visited North Korea from the early 2010s until 2017 to offer medical training to students and professors commented on the level of patriotism among students as they sang and marched around campus as part of their weekly indoctrination session (interviewee #7, interview by the author, December 19, 2014).

---

[47] I conducted sixteen interviews specifically for this Element project between 2016 and 2020. I relied on an additional eleven interviews conducted in 2014 and 2015 from a study on people-to-people engagement in North Korea that were relevant to the current project (see Yeo 2017). With the exception of five interviews conducted over Zoom or voice call due to coronavirus travel restrictions in 2020, all remaining interviews with field-workers or defectors were conducted in person.

[48] Generally two trips per year over a number of years until 2018, when heightened sanctions and travel restrictions (for US citizens) prevented entry into North Korea.

[49] I interacted with these defector students informally for two days during their stay in Washington, DC, in the context of giving lectures on US politics and federalism. Our discussions took place over meals with two NGO volunteers/chaperones.

On the surface, a foreigner would not be aware of North Koreans bringing into question the legitimacy of the regime. To the extent that North Koreans expressed criticism towards the government or specific policies, several field-workers mentioned that their local North Korean counterparts tended to blame corrupt local or provincial officials for economic problems.[50] As one human rights activist, a former professor in North Korea who defected in the early 2000s, stated: North Koreans might criticize provincial leaders, or at times Kim Jong-il, "but rarely did anyone ever criticize the Great Leader (Kim Il-sung)" (interviewee #4, interview by the author, November 21, 2014). The former professor suggested that Kim Il-sung still commanded a high degree of respect and legitimacy from North Koreans, even if his offspring and subsequent leaders did not. In this respect, founding myths remain an important source of legitimacy for the North Korean regime.

Most field-workers I interviewed did not sense that ordinary North Koreans questioned the regime's legitimacy, even if they recognized problems with the socialist system. However, the relative absence of open political criticism does not mean that North Koreans are satisfied with their government when it comes to daily living, despite journalistic accounts of improving economic conditions in Pyongyang and elsewhere (at least until the pandemic). Society's reliance on markets, despite the regime's warnings against capitalism and the risk of punishment, may suggest at least an indirect form of dissent from some North Koreans.

Data from the IPUS surveys from 2011 to 2019 support findings regarding North Koreans' reliance on markets. On average, 70 percent of defectors claimed to have some business experience, with the percentage varying across employment sectors in the following way: 85.5 percent of housewives, 69.9 percent of office clerical workers, 68.6 percent of laborers, 61.8 percent of professionals, 53.6 percent of soldiers, and 48 percent of farmers stated that they had business experience – thus reflecting North Koreans' need (or desire) for additional income, regardless of occupation (IPUS 2020, 31). Opportunities for business in the border regions of North Hamgyong and Ryanggang provinces (where approximately 80 to 90 percent of survey respondents lived when in North Korea) are inevitably higher than in other areas of North Korea. Thus, heavy reliance on markets may not be considered typical of all parts of North Korea. However, even if market and business activities are limited predominantly to border regions and cities, their prevalence suggests either a loosening of state control on market activity or the inability of the regime to strictly regulate

---

[50] This corroborates the finding of other studies using defector interviews (Haggard and Noland 2007; Choi 2013, 661).

economic and social behavior. A field-worker with experience training North Korean entrepreneurs argued that in the past, the regime "vacillated between grudging tolerance and active crackdowns of markets … but in practice the regime has now come to accept markets as a permanent fixture of the North Korea economy" (interviewee #24, interview by the author, May 15, 2020).

4.2 Assessing Markets and Change

Evidence from defector surveys and interviews with field-workers and experts reveals more about North Koreans' reliance on markets than about a realignment of state-society relations. Nevertheless, the data corroborates existing research regarding everyday politics in North Korea (at least as experienced by the defector population), even if North Koreans do not reject *juche* ideology entirely or disapprove of the regime. Although participation in markets does not represent a willful political act of disobedience against the regime, it does suggest greater agency and more interaction among societal actors than might be presumed to exist under a totalitarian regime. Actions which represent "everyday forms of resistance," or "ideological insubordination," such as skipping out on mandatory organizational life (or indoctrination) sessions, accessing foreign media content, or engaging in "capitalistic" and "profit-seeking" enterprises create discursive space, in what political scientist and ethnographer James Scott might describe as "a fairly extensive social existence outside the immediate control of the dominant" (Scott 1990, xi; interviewee #23, interview by the author, April 30, 2020). For sure, market interactions do not constitute civil society, nor do they necessarily create greater autonomy between state and society. However, markets can generate social capital and facilitate trust (Hastings et al. 2021; Kim and Kim 2019). Below I identity two paths for potential societal growth in North Korea, or at the very least, greater discursive space among societal actors that reflects a limited shift in state-society relations.

4.2.1 Between the Private and Public Sphere

Despite the regime's extensive surveillance and monitoring system (see Section 2), the regime is unable to fully dominate everyday life in North Korea. Marketization has produced a semipublic space that exists alongside the authoritarian public sphere. To the extent that markets are only partially regulated, they create space for individual interaction (Kim 2020). Beyond market-related information about the price of goods or business opportunities, topics of discussion may range from the mundane – the weather, current events, and local gossip – to the mildly subversive. North Koreans push the limits of the authoritarian sphere using jokes, humor, and doublespeak to comment on social realities or address regime shortcomings (Park 2018; Joo 2014; Lankov 2013a).

The regime has attempted to combat antirevolutionary behavior and discourse circulating among society through coded language or "hidden transcripts" by shaping the authoritarian public sphere (Dukalskis 2017). Analyzing two decades of *Rodong Sinmun* articles, political scientist Hyungmin Joo (2014) notes the regime's own awareness of what it describes as "corrupt ideology," "decadent culture," and "bourgeois lifestyle" infiltrating the country through movies, songs, books, magazines, radios, the internet, TV programs, USB flash drives, and mobile phone technology (quoted in Joo 2014, 54–55). The regime sees the youth as particularly vulnerable to hidden transcripts that seek to "paralyze class consciousness" and "dilute an independent national spirit" (quoted in Joo 2014, 55). Antisocialist ideas are described as a "dangerous opium" or a "malignant cancer" that will turn North Koreans into "slaves of money" (quoted in Joo 2014, 54–55). The collection of *Rodong Sinmun* articles analyzed by Joo reflects the regime's fear of not only "ideological degeneration" but also the dismantling of the state itself, as a 2011 *Rodong Sinmun* article, translated by Joo, clearly indicates: "When black ink [i.e. antisocialist elements] is poured into water, the color of the water changes and with enough ink, 'pure water' [i.e. North Korea] disappears" (quoted in Joo 2014, 55).

Despite the obvious dangers of being caught with subversive materials, North Koreans have found ways to use or reinterpret official rhetoric in their hidden transcripts to signal discontent with the regime. Several studies relying on defector interviews have revealed similar patterns in the use of coded language and humor, or the appropriation of regime slogans and symbols, to represent the interests of the powerless (Scott 1990). For instance, North Koreans have rephrased the WPK slogan, "If the party decides, we do it," to read, "We do it *no matter what* the party says" (emphasis in original). The play on words reflects the regime's growing irrelevance to the survival of North Koreans (Joo 2014, 56). In another instance of such wordplay, a field-worker interacting closely with North Koreans in China mentioned that young North Koreans might say, "I wish there was a war in North Korea" as a coded way of venting frustration with economic or social conditions in North Korea and hoping for some radical change. But as the field-worker explains, "if you get called out for making such comments, you can always cover your tracks and tell authorities you mean you wanted to see a war so that North Korea can defeat the imperialist Americans" (interviewee #25, interview by the author, June 1, 2020). According to Joo (2010, 133), local markets have become sites of "*malbandong*" (revolution by mouth) where "official rhetoric is increasingly questioned, challenged, and ridiculed by subversive re-interpretation from below." Through hidden transcripts, Joo (2010, 134) finds official regime rhetoric constantly "delegitimized, denaturalized, and de-hegemonized" in North Korean society.

In addition to wordplay, studies based on defector interviews also indicate direct criticism against North Korea's leadership. Haggard and Noland's survey of defectors (2011, 109–11) found that only 8 percent of those surveyed actually complained about the Kim family. However, Joo's (2014) study and the IPUS (2020) surveys suggest criticism against the regime rose steadily under Kim Jong-il. Although referred to as the Dear Leader in public, Joo (2014, 59) found that defectors rarely used this honorific title for Kim Jong-il in their conversation, instead mentioning him as "that guy" or other more derogatory names. Such criticism peaked around the time of the botched 2009 currency reform. Joo (2014, 60) and others speculated at the time that "character assassination" of leaders would continue, stating, "judging from their content, it seems that the grandfather (Kim Il-Sung) was beloved, the father (Kim Jong-Il) is hated, and the son (Kim Jong-Un) will be ridiculed." This may certainly have been the case initially, especially given Kim Jong-un's youth and inexperience. However, by taking on a more personable and public persona similar to his grandfather (Kim Il-sung), rather than his more reserved father (Kim Jong-il), Kim Jong-un seems to have shored up his legitimacy as reflected in the IPUS surveys (see Figure 7).

Beyond discourse, nonverbal signals and actions can also be interpreted as indirect challenges to government authority. For instance, some see the shift in women's fashion, influenced by foreign fashion sensibilities, as a public statement against the social mores promoted by the regime (Saucedo 2020; Giacomo 2017). Consumption of foreign movies, TV shows, music, and, most notably, South Korean popular culture, while not necessarily an act of deliberate subversion, are in direct violation of North Korean law.

Marketization has brought greater consumerism and materialism in North Korea that can be witnessed in everyday practices. As one former business owner in Rason shared, "with growing markets, there are obvious changes on the ground in Rason such as the construction of high-rise apartments, and also a growing demand for money ... some [North Koreans] with money are even flipping houses in Rason" (interviewee #16, interview by the author, June 6, 2019). In another anecdote, the same business owner shared how after serious floods destroyed hundreds of homes, including the home of one of his employees, the government offered to rebuild everyone's home for free to demonstrate the benevolence of the North Korean regime.[51] As the business owner remarks,

---

[51] The DPRK government touted the construction of "new modern dwelling houses under socialism" built by soldiers after homes were destroyed by a typhoon in 2020 (DPRK Today 2020).

however, "the quality of housing turned out to be extremely poor, and my employee mentioned he needed a better door, better insulation, and that things were breaking. I don't know to what extent it was a tact to get money from me, but the point is North Koreans are demanding more and they want better things for themselves" (interviewee #16, interview by the author, June 6, 2019).

Another field-worker in the Rason region, discussing hiring practices at his business, mentioned that North Korean companies hired a large number of people but work was not always readily available. Pay was often low compared to other foreign-owned companies. Workers in state-owned factories therefore looked for side jobs. North Koreans did not criticize or blame the government for these shortcomings, but as field-workers pointed out, workers were often searching for more and better opportunities that offered higher income (interviewee #10, interview by the author, October 24, 2015). A business owner in Rason mentioned that he would receive requests from his workers and their acquaintances asking if their daughters could also be hired into his company, since foreign firms had a reputation for treating their employees better than North Korean firms (interviewee #16, interview by the author, June 6, 2019).

While North Koreans may outwardly extoll the virtues of their socialist paradise, in practice, many are fully engaged in capitalist behavior. In the words of Hassig and Oh (2015, 2), "The North Korean people are no longer socialist . . . they are instead free-market capitalists." Choi and Roh (2008, 102) go so far as to argue that *juche* is now dead, replaced by materialism and the ideology of survival. North Koreans sought "individual survival in the name of 'autonomy' rather than obedience to the state" (Choi 2013, 665). Facing starvation during the Arduous March, Choi (2013, 665) writes that "socialist principles and the spirit of collectivism could no longer control the ordinary residents, and eventually the most basic desire of survival clashed with socialist collectivism." More candid expressions of "individual desire" have continued to emerge in the Kim Jong-un era (Park et al. 2018, 273–74).

Antirevolutionary behavior, including capital accumulation and consumption, has drawn the attention of party leaders. In contrast to official narratives that proclaim that citizens remain faithful to the socialist revolution, editorials in the *Rodong Sinmun* chide North Koreans who have become "slaves of money" or "blinded by greed"; these are "betrayers of the revolution, willing to sell their country for a few dollars" (*Rodong Sinmun*, quoted in Joo 2014, 61). From the mid-2000s, the regime ramped up efforts to regulate markets and curb the scourge of capitalism through propaganda, reeducation, and self-criticism sessions.[52]

---

[52] See, for example, an article from January 2019 in the *Rodong Sinmun* titled "Capitalist Society Has No Future" (Ri 2019).

Paradoxically, the symbiotic relationship between state and markets has also meant that "the daily practices of local Party officials" also "promoted, legitimized, and valorized market dynamics" despite officials contradicting their own party's message (Smith 2015, 212). Underpaid government officials have all the more incentive to ignore violations or reduce penalties for those caught breaking the law in exchange for bribes, thereby weakening the coercive apparatus of the state. As one Chinese scholar who frequently visits North Korea disclosed,

> The *inminbanjang* (neighborhood watch head) who is responsible for 30 to 40 families in the neighborhood is supposed to report or punish anyone in the community who appears disloyal or is breaking the law or involved in antistate activity. However, *inminbanjang* also knows the importance of markets so she may not enforce rules. Or even worse, she may accept a bribe if those under her jurisdiction are making money from markets (interviewee #21, interview by the author, December 2019).

As Hazel Smith (2015, 212) argues, "the Party became the driver and *de facto* legitimator of marketization and in so doing ceased to act as a well-functioning, reliable transmission belt for ideological education and revolutionary discipline." The party still functions as a powerful organization and wields significant authority. However, it has become "less feared as an instrument of state control" from the days of Kim Il-sung, with officials less likely to undercut their own economic interests (Smith 2015, 220).

Market activity has also helped channel information from the outside world into North Korea as North Koreans interact with traders from China and elsewhere. As Jieun Baek (2016, xviii) argues, "the active flow of goods and information now plays a central role in the social consciousness of North Korean individuals." The relationship between information about the outside world – whether obtained through markets or via foreign intervention – and the erosion of the authoritarian public sphere is not automatic. However, foreign media and the knowledge they bring about the outside world can create cognitive dissonance, causing some North Koreans to question the regime. As Baek (2016, 79) finds in her interviews with defectors, North Koreans repeatedly exposed to outside information face a "mental tug-of-war between pro-regime beliefs on one side, and disbelief and skepticism on the other." Exposure to foreign media or engaging in illicit market activity does not necessarily alter North Koreans' perception of the regime, or lead to their disavowal of *juche* ideology – as attested by the IPUS survey data. At the same time, however, market participants have ditched much of the formal economy – a core pillar of the communist state – in favor of "capitalistic practices." Outwardly they praise the regime, but privately they act or speak in ways inconsistent with revolutionary ideals.

Social change, including the rise of an autonomous public sphere, rarely progresses in a linear fashion. The "military first" era of Kim Jong-il was marked by decreasing support and increasing criticism of the regime leadership, leading some analysts to speculate a continuing downward trajectory under Kim Jong-un. However, North Koreans appear less critical of the current Kim Jong-un leadership, perhaps due to a combination of the younger Kim's greater charisma, his support for economic development, and tighter messaging regarding his foreign policy achievements – including his historic 2018 meeting with US president Donald Trump in Singapore. The policy shift from the *songun* (military first) to the *byungjin* line, along with structural changes and personnel reshuffling within the politburo, the Central Military Commission, and the cabinet, may suggest institutional adaptation on the part of the regime and its efforts to steer or co-opt markets in a direction which minimizes dissent.

However, evidence from defectors does suggest "hotspots" for social change in the border regions where markets and knowledge about the outside world are more widespread (Park 2018). Although the defector population does not represent North Korean society at large, their collective input suggests a concentration of wealth in Pyongyang and a few other cities, and a limited degree of social mobility among a new class of economic elites (Kretchun and Kim 2012, 44). Market participants with greater access to outside information in these hotspots exhibit a growing gap in rhetoric and behavior between the private and public spheres. Through jokes and euphemisms addressing shortcomings, criticisms aimed at government officials, and foreign media content circulated among family members, friends, and other market participants, North Koreans have managed to carve out a semipublic space outside of the regime's strategy of domination. Some defectors have even reported that their *inminban* – the very mechanism created by the regime to reinforce the revolutionary spirit at the most local level – had become a space for watching foreign media content together (Williams 2019, 14).

Whether cognizant of such actions or not, North Koreans that choose to skip out on organizational life meetings or take days off from their official sector job in favor of other business opportunities are also partaking in everyday resistance. Ironically, the state has become an enabler and complicit in supporting antirevolutionary behavior by adopting legal measures such as the July 1, 2002 special measures or the Socialist Enterprise Responsibility Management System (SERMS) in 2014, and tolerating illegal acts such as bribery and corruption that allow "capitalistic practices" to thrive.[53] Of course, the regime implemented "reforms" to sustain, not replace, the socialist system (Kim 2014).

---

[53] SERMS, which was officially announced by Kim Jong-un on May 30, 2014, provided SOEs greater management autonomy and latitude in how profits might be utilized (Gray and Lee 2021, 182).

However, such measures are a tacit acknowledgement of existing market realities and an effort on the regime's part to legitimize practices that may have once been deemed antirevolutionary. In this vein, marketization has the potential to "diminish the authority and legitimacy of the leadership" (Smith 2015, 213). As market-based networks and private information sharing expand, they may gradually spill into the public sphere, inadvertently unveiling the hidden transcripts that had previously been camouflaged behind the pomp, pageantry, and performative practices required of citizens by the regime (Wedeen 2015, 148).

4.2.2 Markets and Trust Networks

In addition to a widening gap between private thoughts and public discourse, market activity, particularly at the level of the general markets, fosters horizontal trust networks among market participants. Selling and buying in markets often lends itself to building social networks for sharing information, finding new business opportunities, building trust, and decreasing transactional uncertainty. These networks are maintained face-to-face, but also through mobile phone contact (Kim 2019). Buyers and sellers may be opportunistic and motivated purely by self-interest and profit. However, repeated interactions help reduce uncertainty and develop trust. Over time, multiple transactions with buyers and sellers in a local market produces knowledge about prices, transportation routes, the reputation of sellers and buyers and their products, and other pieces of information relevant to sustaining markets. This knowledge exists in the public sphere to the extent that it is shared among participants who have developed a sufficient degree of social trust through market exchanges. For instance, one field-worker described, as follows, how business and financial transactions continued during the pandemic despite strict lockdowns:

> No one trusts North Korea's banking system. But if you want to send money or make a financial transaction or purchase, you give the money to a *donju*. The *donju* then transfers money [via cellphone or by traversing borders] to the intended recipient, or to another *donju* near the recipient to provide funds. The *donju* are able to cross the country [presumably through their political connections], so they can deliver goods or transfer money between people. Some North Koreans were even sending money for funerals through *donju* during the lockdown (interviewee #10, follow-up phone interview by the author, January 7, 2021).

The same field-worker mentioned that conducting business in North Korea is like the "wild West in that there are no clear or formal rules" (interviewee #10, follow-up phone interview by the author, January 7, 2021). As such, financial and other market transactions require an element of trust among market participants. Market participants themselves determine what behavior is acceptable or not by retaliating against cheaters or publicly outing bad actors, thereby creating informal rules and practices. The trust networks emerging from market activity cannot be equated with civil society. However, market-oriented trust networks can promote social capital as entrepreneurs and traders work in pursuit of a common goal, even if ultimately motivated by self-interest and profit.

To cope with constant uncertainty given the absence of formal rules or contracts, vendors and distributors must rely on informal trust networks to operate businesses (Cho and Yim 2008, 273–78). They turn to family, friends, or neighbors with experience in markets, or seek personal connections to local government and/or party officials (interviewee #27, interview by the author, November 10, 2020). Large-scale merchants operating in urban areas have built business networks in several regions throughout North Korea and "exchanged information about exchange rates and prices with merchants in other regions," cooperatively adjusting the price of goods with other merchants (Choi 2013, 659).

Networks also extend to the state sector as merchants regularly pay bribes to the military and SOEs to use their state-registered vehicles to transport goods across the country for their "private" business (Choi 2013, 659). Bribery and corruption itself is embedded in the market system with cases of local officials referring *donju* to other officials (Kim 2017). Market traders have even reported building network opportunities while kept in detention after getting caught for illegal market behavior (Choi 2013, 660). Although most North Korea experts and journalists tend to focus on the rising economic power of the *donju*, a field-worker with experience conducting academic exchanges with North Korea was quick to note the embedded nature of market and state actors. As the field-worker argued, "the *donju* don't have their own independent power base. They can't fight the state so they became *donju* to work together with the state. The *donju* [and the regime] rise and fall together" (interviewee #26, interview by the author, June 5, 2020).

Although state officials are embedded in market networks, particularly when involving large volume transactions or in the real estate and finance sectors, institutional knowledge regarding markets is more likely held by private rather than state actors. For instance, a field-worker knowledgeable about North Korean entrepreneurship stated that government officials were often unfamiliar with formal, much less informal guidelines regulating business. North Koreans seeking to start a new business instead sought advice on navigating bureaucratic rules from other private entrepreneurs (interviewee #27, interview by the author, November 10, 2020).

Market actors within a given network may be motivated by self-interest. Nevertheless, mutual exchanges repeated over time can produce trust. Of course, as stated above, informal market networks are not equivalent to civil society, and most networks remain private and limited in scale (Haggard et al. 2012). However, if market-based interactions can extend to relationships that go beyond business transactions, or if exchanging information about goods and prices encourages discussion about other nonmarket-related topics such as current events, fashion trends, or even neighborhood gossip, market activity may indirectly give shape to a public sphere.

Finally, markets have shifted how information flows between state and society. In the era of the command economy, "the structure of information circulation in North Korea was planned, produced, and monopolized by the party and state organizations" (Choi 2013, 661). Information flowed vertically from the top down through the party system to local organizations. As Choi (2013, 661) argues, "Such a unilateral system implied that there was no information or feedback flowing from society to the state, but rather only a unidirectional flow from the state to society." However, markets have weakened the state's monopoly over control and content of information. State and societal actors seek out information from markets relevant to survival. The prices of gas, cooking oil, rice, sugar, and other staples – although set by the state – are often adjusted to market prices. Information about transportation routes, new regulations and their enforcement, the reputation of merchants, and news from China and South Korea about the outside world are circulated through market networks (interviewee #10, interview by the author, October 24, 2015).

4.3 Conclusion

Market forces have led to a shift in state-society relations as North Koreans simultaneously employ "strategies of obedience, deviation, resistance, and compromise" on a daily basis against the regime (Choi 2013, 656). Market dynamics have also facilitated the rise of informal trust networks, allowing information and resources to flow horizontally, and, in the case of public-private partnerships, vertically. Although our understanding of North Korea is limited by methodological and data constraints, insights from defector surveys and interviews, as well as additional insights from North Korea field-workers and experts, do shed some light on societal attitudes towards the regime. While defector surveys point to limited support for the regime and its ideology, additional sources indicate a gap between public and private thoughts about the regime and a weakening of "official norms, rules, and institutions" as the regime adapts to "new social realities" (Dukalskis and Joo 2020, 1).

The ability of North Koreans to "muddle through" is a testament to their resourcefulness and entrepreneurialism. Underneath the authoritarian public sphere, North Koreans have found ways to cope with economic shortages and hardships by building and relying on their own networks, and using hidden transcripts to share common experiences and air criticism. For sure, the regime continues to clamp down on the rights and freedoms of North Koreans. Yet, the problem of legitimacy abounds in North Korea as attested by frequent exhortations in the official state media to reject the rising scourge of capitalism, and corroborated by defectors' reports of acts of criticism, shirking, and other antirevolutionary behavior. To argue that state-society relations have shifted does not mean that North Koreans are ready to partake in mass revolution, but it does suggest more room for North Koreans to maneuver within the authoritarian public sphere.

5 Conclusion: Contingency and Change in North Korea

In an effort to understand state-society relations in North Korea, this Element has focused almost entirely on the country's internal dynamics. In this concluding section, I first recapitulate the main hypotheses and findings in the context of understanding change in North Korea. I then address how North Korea's foreign relations and other external factors influence market dynamics and state-society relations. Just as North Korea's current nuclear stance and foreign policy isolation (both by choice and foreign imposition) are likely to perpetuate the status quo, a diplomatic breakthrough with the USA and the international community may also open a window for more significant domestic change.

5.1 Reviewing State-Society Relations in North Korea

Evaluating change in state-society relations in North Korea is difficult. Aside from problems with access to reliable data, the country itself poses several contradictions. For example, despite numerous accounts from defectors, journalists, and foreign travelers that reveal a fair degree of economic and social change in North Korea (at least for specific segments of the population), the country still remains one of the poorest and most authoritarian in the world, suggesting little change on the surface.

As described in Section 2, one notable change has been the rise of the market economy, including the growth of informal markets, and greater decentralization of the command economy. Economic change, in turn, has produced limited social change for the middle class with additional disposable income earned through markets. The *nouveau riche* in Pyongyang, including the *donju*, have experienced greater social change marked by access to new technology such as smartphones and tablets, which help increase their knowledge about the outside world (Lankov 2013b). More importantly, marketization has facilitated new interdependent relationships between private entrepreneurs and state bureaucrats that were nonexistent until the 2000s, thus indicating some shift in state-society dynamics.

In contrast to limited economic and social changes in North Korea, there are very few signs of political change. While the Supreme Leader may have replaced older party cadres with younger leaders, and given support to policies that expand foreign trade opportunities and marketization, initial speculation that Kim Jong-un might be a reformer has proven to be inaccurate as the Supreme Leader has thus far shunned the reformist path. Potential reformers within the upper ranks of the WPK have yet to surface since the execution of Kim's uncle, Jang Song-thaek, in 2013 (Mansourov 2013).

Shaped by modernization theory and the devolution of Soviet-backed communist parties in Eastern Europe, the prediction that marketization might lead to modest political reforms is a familiar one, although it has not been borne out in communist Asia. For instance, addressing the effects of marketization on state-society relations in China in the mid-2000s, political scientist Bruce Dickson (2007, 827) described the prevailing sentiment at the time as follows:

> The increased economic and political prominence of private entrepreneurs has received special attention from scholars and also Western media. Some note the potential for China's new economic elites to serve as agents of change, either by subtly influencing the CCP from within or engaging in organized collective action against the state on economic and political issues. Others see private entrepreneurs as the leading edge of an emerging civil society that will eventually transform China's political system.

Marketization in North Korea approaches nowhere near the levels of China's market economy in the 2000s. Nevertheless, Dickson's remarks with regard to China parallel the cautious optimism expressed by Western observers regarding changes that had emerged in North Korea prior to the escalation of international sanctions in 2016. As with the Chinese Communist Party (CCP), however, the WPK adopted limited economic "measures"[54] without any intention of relaxing its political control. Organizational life sessions, daily surveillance, and ideological indoctrination have all persisted in the Kim Jong-un era. Despite the reported closure (or merger) of one or two major political prison camps, the gulags run by the MSS continue to operate. In response to new information

---

[54] The North Korean government avoids using the term "reform."

technologies, the regime has also adapted its surveillance and censorship methods to block illegal content on smartphones and laptops.[55]

Underneath the authoritarian public sphere, however, perceptions about the outside world, and perhaps indirectly the regime and its ideology, have shifted with increased exposure to markets and foreign information. Market interactions have also generated horizontal ties and helped build a modicum of trust among sellers and buyers that ultimately enable markets to flourish, despite North Korea's inhospitable business climate (Kim and Lee 2019). Even under the threat of repression, North Koreans have found ways to ignore and circumvent existing rules. Horizontal networks, especially those characterized by corruption, have generated regime concerns about institutional weakening and moral decay from the party as evidenced by periodic crackdowns directed against the *donju* and corrupt officials, and public decrees reminding citizens of the corrupting effects of capitalism.[56]

It is too early to fully comprehend the impact of rising markets on state-society relations or its implications for the Kim family dynasty. I have argued that if the state is unable to co-opt markets into its regime ideology, markets may create a further gap between state and society by empowering societal actors, including private entrepreneurs, vis-à-vis the state. At least until 2016, this appeared to be the trend. Although the regime periodically instituted measures to bring markets to heel, it ultimately expanded official foreign trade and permitted private businesses and investments to grow. These factors contributed to modest economic growth in North Korea's economy during the first five years of Kim Jong-un's rule (with the exception of 2015).[57] As markets grow, so too will market-centered associational life – that is, the horizontal trust networks that develop both within and outside of the state's official purview. Unless the state manages to incorporate markets into its broader regime narrative and co-opt the development of this unofficial "civil society," the regime may face increasing instability. Greater demand for information, transparency, and stable property rights, as well as increased interaction among market traders, will erode the regime's grip over society.

Some may reject this prediction against the backdrop of China's experience with marketization *sans* political liberalization (Tsai 2007). However, this ignores the reality of the changed nature of state-society relations in China,

---

[55] This includes platforms which run surveillance and file integrity checks such as Red Star and Trace Viewer, and relying on file watermarking and digital signatures (Williams 2019, 34–37).

[56] Similar concerns regarding corruption have played out in China (Greitens 2020).

[57] Between 2012 to 2016, BOK estimates indicate North Korea's economy grew anywhere between 1 to 3.9 percent. In 2015, however, the economy shrank by 1.1 percent. These figures are derived by the author from BOK statistics (Economics Statistics System, Bank of Korea, http://ecos.bok.or.kr/flex/ClassSearch.jsp?langGubun=K&topCode=I01Y001).

especially if one reflects back to the era of Mao Zedong – which North Korea's personalist dictatorship more closely resembles today. Even if state authority has not receded, the nature of state-society relations in China has transformed during the last four decades. As Mary Gallagher (2004, 423) states:

> The depoliticization of daily life, the decline of ideology, the expansion of the private and non-state sectors in the economy, the opening to foreign trade, investment, and influence, the withdrawal of the state from key functions such as labor allocation and certain aspects of social welfare – all have radically changed the way Chinese people live, work, and interact with one another and with state and party authorities ... A consumer revolution has taken place among urban Chinese, leading to a rapid expansion in domestic tourism, fashion, the arts, and other interests that had been severely restricted in the late Maoist period.

North Korea, or at least a certain segment of an "enlightened" population, appeared to be moving along this path of social awakening – at least until the country was hit with heavy economic sanctions, and then by the global pandemic in 2020, which has extended into 2021.

Drawing on China's experience, then, a shift in state-society relations spurred by marketization does not necessarily mean the beginning of the end for the regime. There is a strong Western tendency to see civil society as a correlative of democracy and so to assume that economic liberalization and the rise of private actors will inevitably lead to democratic governance. China's state-corporatist model offers important comparative lessons, despite major differences in the origins and scope of marketization between China and North Korea. In China, the growth of civic associations is not an indication of receding state power, but "an evolution away from direct state control to indirect state coordination" (Gallagher 2004, 420). Scholars have also weighed in on the state-corporatist model by pointing to a "semi-civil society" or "state-led civil society" (Gallagher 2004, 420). Markets may thus occupy a space between state and society that is "constituted by both, but subsumed by neither" (Gallagher 2004, 421). This insight is apt for North Korea. Given the existing mutual interdependence between the *donju* and SOEs in North Korea, there is reason to believe that the Kim family may eventually follow China's corporatist path.[58]

To co-opt civil society and markets, North Korea would need to integrate markets and incorporate elements of capitalism within its regime ideology. North Korea's leadership still appears unprepared to embrace market dynamics into its official regime narrative as North Korean propaganda routinely and

---

[58] As Gallagher (2004, 421) argues, the state interacts with associational groups through "mutual penetration, converging interests, and co-optation" rather than violence or repression.

vehemently reject all forms of capitalism. It is worth noting that following the Tiananmen Square protests in 1989, the CCP also distanced itself from capitalism by banning the recruitment of private entrepreneurs into their ranks. According to Bruce Dickson (2020), this made ideological sense since capitalists were the alleged "class enemies of communists." However, the CCP quickly learned that the ban "conflict[ed] with local political realities because party and government officials needed cooperation from private entrepreneurs" (Dickson 2020). As Dickson (2020) argues, CCP leaders soon recognized the need to update the official ideology "to match the unofficial practice of co-opting entrepreneurs into the party." To this end, the CCP claimed that entrepreneurs (referred to as "advanced productive force") also belonged to the revolutionary class along with workers, farmers, and soldiers. Dickson's observations about Chinese state participation in markets reflects a dilemma that the WPK and Kim regime may eventually have to resolve. In particular, North Korean officials and SOE managers must rely on the private sector to maintain the economy and to secure their own position. To iron out ideological contradictions and sustain the regime's legitimacy, the WPK may thus need to rework its ideology to frame markets as a manifestation of *juche*.

Some have argued that the Kim regime has already updated its official narrative in light of social and economic changes by introducing policies which place a greater emphasis on "civilian economic growth" (i.e. bottom-up marketization). These policy measures include the July 1, 2002 Economic Management Improvement Measure and the June 28, 2012 New Economic Management Measure promoted by Kim Jong-un (Park 2019). It is possible that the regime's recent emphasis on "our style socialism" (*Rodong Sinmun* 2020b) or "economic management in our style" (Yonhap 2017) may, in fact, create sufficient discursive space to include markets within the framework of *juche*, especially if "our style" taps into the ingenuity, resourcefulness, and entrepreneurial spirit of the North Korean people represented by bottom-up marketization. Kim Jong-un's public appearances at local businesses and factories, construction sites, collective farms, and various ribbon-cutting ceremonies sustains the belief that the Supreme Leader oversees all economic development, regardless of whether production (and profit) are driven by official or unofficial means. Again, it is too early to know whether Kim Jong-un can successfully integrate capitalist practices with "our style" socialism. Based on the experience of other communist regimes, however, North Korean leaders will need to follow through with ideological as well as institutional adaptation (Dimitrov 2013) to secure their rule should markets further empower societal actors.

5.2 External Relations and Exogenous Factors

The difficulty in theorizing state-society relations, much less making predictions about North Korea's future, also rests on several external relationships and factors. US-North Korea relations during the Trump administration (2017–2021) lurched between the brink of "fire and fury" and unprecedented diplomatic engagement between Chairman Kim and President Trump in Singapore and Hanoi in 2018 and 2019, respectively. Unfortunately for both sides, the euphoria surrounding a renewed US-North Korea relationship evaporated after the failure of the Hanoi Summit. Bilateral relations came to a standstill for the remainder of the Trump-Kim era.

During the Singapore Summit, Trump relayed to Kim a four-minute video trailer promising a "new world," replete with foreign investment opportunities, medical breakthroughs, abundant resources, and technological innovations (Stewart 2018). Whether Kim will "advance his country and be part of a new world? Be the hero of his people?" as posed by the narrator, is not a decision that can be decided by the North Korean leader alone. Heavy sanctions imposed by the United States and the international community prevent North Korea from realizing economic progress, including further market reforms and economic development. North Korea is also unlikely to receive assistance from international lending banks such as the International Monetary Fund or the World Bank without first taking steps to abandon its nuclear weapons program. Most foreign companies are also deterred from investing in North Korea without the guarantee of property rights and the rule of law. Yet, North Korea faces difficult trade-offs and cannot simply negotiate away its nuclear weapons, which the regime sees as critical for maintaining external security as well as domestic legitimacy. Nor can it readily loosen social control over the population. Even with tighter sanctions enforcement, it therefore appears unlikely that North Korea will commit to denuclearization.

China remains North Korea's most important patron, and – until COVID-19 – accounted for 95 percent of North Korea's foreign trade (Koen and Beom 2020, 24). China has and will continue to play a significant role in North Korea's formal and informal economy. Beijing would like nothing more than for North Korea to follow its lead in transitioning to a market economy and transforming into a stable buffer state between itself and the US military stationed in South Korea (Bodeen 2019; Albert 2019). To follow China's lead, however, would require expanding foreign trade and investment significantly, thereby opening relations with the outside world. Such a move would weaken the regime's ability to control information, posing risks to the legitimacy of the Kim family dynasty. Although China is capable of providing more assistance to North

Korea, its hands are tied (at least in the legal realm) due to the international sanctions regime. However, Beijing's enforcement of sanctions has at best been uneven and a constant source of US ire. It is important to note that China does not condone North Korea's nuclear weapons program due to its destabilizing effect on the region. For that reason, Beijing will continue to give lip service to sanctions and limit its economic support for North Korea.

South Korea's Moon Jae-in government has been extremely keen to resume relations with North Korea. The progressive Moon government has expended enormous energy and capital to jump-start diplomatic engagement since coming to office in 2017. President Moon's diplomatic outreach appeared to bear some fruit with three inter-Korea summits held between Moon and Chairman Kim in 2018. President Moon also helped orchestrate an impromptu meeting between Kim and President Trump at the demilitarized zone during Trump's visit to South Korea in June 2019. Despite Moon's efforts, however, much of the diplomatic goodwill fizzled once US-North Korea diplomacy grinded to a halt. The Moon government has been consistent in its willingness to jump-start humanitarian assistance and dialogue with North Korea, but Seoul has been constantly rebuffed by Pyongyang. To make its point, North Korea detonated the inter-Korea liaison office located in Kaesong in June 2020, allegedly in response to activists launching balloons into North Korea with antiregime messages. The Moon government is eager to be a key partner in North Korea's future economic development. However, North Korea clearly prioritizes its relationship with Washington over Seoul, thus limiting South Korea's ability to encourage North Korea to follow the path of denuclearization and reforms. South Korean efforts to promote inter-Korea engagement have also been significantly constrained by UN and US sanctions.

In sum, although the relationship between state, society, and markets in North Korea is fundamentally domestic in nature, whether marketization can proceed remains contingent on North Korea's relationship with external actors. Will the United States settle for disarmament and arms control rather than denuclearization as a condition for rolling back sanctions? To what extent is China willing to enforce sanctions or offer the Kim regime political cover? Will inter-Korea projects such as an inter-Korea railway or humanitarian and development assistance create a virtuous cycle, opening Pyongyang to greater international cooperation and additional foreign investment? A return to the cautious optimism regarding markets and state-society relations during the first few years of Kim Jong-un's rule is unlikely until sanctions are rolled back. Even then, however, sanctions relief will not guarantee economic improvement. More meaningful, positive domestic changes are thus dependent on several international factors. This includes renewed diplomatic efforts with the international community, and in particular, with the United States.

5.3 The Impact of COVID-19

Beyond nuclear weapons, sanctions, and foreign relations, the COVID-19 pandemic has become the most defining factor affecting markets, state, and society in recent years, and will carry repercussions for at least the next year or two. North Korea was the first country to shut down its borders in response to Beijing's announcement of the coronavirus in January 2020. The strict border lockdown has all but eliminated Sino-North Korea trade. Chinese customs data indicated trade levels decreasing between 2019 and 2020 by 75 to 80 percent (Choy 2020). Chinese official exports to North Korea in November 2020 amounted to US$148,000 – a figure far from the nearly US$200 million in exports in November 2019 (Choy 2020).[59] Unofficial trade and smuggling has also likely plummeted due to strict border controls. North Korean markets and private businesses have undoubtedly been adversely affected given their heavy reliance on cross-border trade.

As discussed in Section 3, during the pandemic lockdown, the state restricted movement and imposed quarantines as part of its COVID-19 response. However, the regime has also used the border lockdown as an opportunity to reestablish its authority over markets by cracking down on private entrepreneurs and corrupt officials, and also restricting the use of foreign currency (Ward 2020; Wertz 2020). A key question is whether the regime's recent moves are merely temporary measures in response to COVID-19 to reduce market activity (as a means of preventing mass outbreaks, which the country's low health care capacity would be unable to handle) and raise much-needed cash, or if they represent a longer term trend to walk back private commerce and align unofficial markets to the formal economy. Either way, economic recovery and the resumption of trade to pre-COVID-19 levels will take time due to the major disruptions in supply chain and logistics networks caused by the lockdown.

North Korea has muddled through crises before. Ordinary North Koreans are thus arguably better prepared today than during the Arduous March to confront a humanitarian crisis as North Koreans have now learned *not* to rely on the state. Beyond coping with COVID-19 hardships, it remains to be seen whether the regime decides to reembrace markets and lean on private capital to help

---

[59] Chinese customs data can be accessed at "Total Value of Imported and Exported Goods," Report on Statistics, General Administration of Customs of the People's Republic of China, December 23, 2020, www.customs.gov.cn/customs/302249/zfxxgk/2799825/302274/302277/302276/3479983/index.html.

jump-start the economy once the pandemic subsides. Doing so may require some degree of rapprochement with the USA to allow for partial sanctions relief, which in turn may again shift relations between state, society, and markets in North Korea.

5.4 Conclusion

The relationship between state, society, and markets in North Korea is not an academic question. At stake are the lives of 26 million North Koreans. A small percentage of the population may be well-off economically by some global standards. However, the majority live a spartan, if not a meager, existence shaped by profound restrictions. Even prior to the humanitarian crisis caused by the pandemic, a March 2019 UN report found that 43 percent of the population, or 11 million North Koreans, were "food insecure" with one in five children experiencing stunted growth as a result of chronic malnutrition (UN Resident Coordinator 2019, 3, 25). Although average North Koreans may live normal lives (Kang 2012), as Barbara Demick (2009) observes there is certainly "nothing to envy."

The international community, and especially South Korea, would like nothing more than to see North Korea follow the path of denuclearization, marketization, and reform. Unfortunately, the path to reform remains entangled, or perhaps ensnared, in security politics and seven decades of the Kim family doing things "our way." As with most personalist dictatorships, the safer path has been adherence to the status quo rather than innovation and modernization. Market growth may not be the answer to all of North Korea's problems; however, it does illuminate a path for reshaping state-society relations in a manner that offers North Koreans better opportunities than what the regime is currently capable of providing.

References

Abrahamian, A. (2020). *Being in North Korea*. Stanford, CA: Shorenstein Asia-Pacific Research Center.

Abrahamian, A. & See, G. (2014). *The ABCs of North Korea's SEZs*. Washington, DC: US-Korea Institute at SAIS.

Alagappa, M. (2004). *Civil Society and Political Change in Asia: Expanding and Contracting Democratic Space*. Stanford, CA: Stanford University Press.

Albert, E. (2019). "The China-North Korea Relationship." Council on Foreign Relations. Last updated June 25. www.cfr.org/backgrounder/china-north-korea-relationship.

Arendt, H. (1951). *The Origins of Totalitarianism*. New York: Schocken Books.

Armstrong, C. K. (2013). Ideological Introversion and Regime Survival: North Korea's 'Our-Style Socialism.' In M. K. Dimitrov, ed., *Why Communism Did Not Collapse: Understanding Authoritarian Regime Resilience in Asia and Europe*. Cambridge: Cambridge University Press, 99–119.

Associated Press. (2020). "North Korean Leader Kim Jong-un Acknowledges Economic Shortfalls amid COVID-19, Flooding and Heavy Sanctions." ABC News. August 21. www.abc.net.au/news/2020-08-21/north-korean-leader-kim-jong-un-acknowledges-economic-shortfalls/12582622.

Babson, B. (2020). "The North Korean Economy under Sanctions and Covid-19." 38 North, May 22. www.38north.org/2020/05/bbabson052220/.

Baek, J. (2016). *North Korea's Hidden Revolution: How the Information Underground Is Transforming a Closed Society*. New Haven, CT: Yale University Press.

Bendix, R., Bendix, J. & Furniss, N. (1987). Reflections on Modern Western States and Civil Societies. In R. G. Braungart & M. M. Braungart, eds., *Research in Political Sociology*. Volume 3. London: JAI Press, 1–38.

Bodeen, C. (2019). "China's Xi Pushes Economic Reform at North Korea Summit." Associated Press, June 21. https://apnews.com/article/weapons-programs-ap-top-news-north-korea-international-news-nuclear-weapons-8d5f00b17403495db198e993aeb1c73c.

Bueno de Mesquita, B. & Smith, A. (2011). *The Dictator's Handbook: Why Bad Behavior Is Almost Always Good Politics*. New York: PublicAffairs.

Byman, D. & Lind, J. (2010). Pyongyang's Survival Strategy: Tools of Authoritarian Control in North Korea. *International Security* 35(1), 44–74.

Byrne, T. & Corrado, J. (2019). *Making North Korea Creditworthy: What Will It Take to Finance Its Post-Nuclear Development?* New York: Korea Society.

Cha, V. D. & Anderson, N. D. (2012). A North Korean Spring? *Washington Quarterly* 35(1), 7–24.

Cha, V. D. & Collins, L. (2018). "The Markets: Private Economy and Capitalism in North Korea?" Beyond Parallel, Center for Strategic and International Studies. August 26. https://beyondparallel.csis.org/markets-private-economy-capitalism-north-korea/.

Choe, S. H. (2019). "North Korea's State-Run Economy Falters under Sanctions, Testing Elite Loyalty." *New York Times*, April 18. www .nytimes.com/2019/04/18/world/asia/north-korea-economy-sanctions.html.

Choe, S. H. (2020a). "In North Korea, Coronavirus Hurts More Than Any Sanctions Could." *New York Times*, July 4. www.nytimes.com/2020/07/04/ world/asia/north-korea-sanctions-coronavirus.html.

Choe, S. H. (2020b). "North Korea's Leader Had Big Economic Plans. He Admits They've Failed." *New York Times*, August 19. www.nytimes.com /2020/08/19/world/asia/north-korea-economy-coronavirus.html.

Choi, C. (2013). 'Everyday Politics' in North Korea. *The Journal of Asian Studies* 72(3), 655–73.

Choi, W. K. & Roh, G. N. (2008). Bukhan jumin ui sajeok yongman [North Koreans' personal desires]. In W. Y. Lee, ed., *Bukhan dosijuminui sajeok yeongyeok yungu* [A study on the private lives of North Korean urban dwellers]. Seoul: Hanul.

Choy, M. C. (2020). "North Korea's Trade with China Free Falls in November, Reaching New Record Lows." *NK Pro*, December 24. www.nknews.org/pro/ north-koreas-trade-with-china-free-falls-in-november-reaching-new-record-lows/.

Coleman, J. S. (1990). *Foundations of Social Theory*. Cambridge, MA: Harvard University Press.

Collins, R. M. (2012). *Marked for Life: Songbun, North Korea's Social Classification System*. Washington, DC: Committee for Human Rights in North Korea.

Collins, R. M. (2018). *Denied from the Start: Human Rights at the Local Level in North Korea*. Washington, DC: Committee for Human Rights in North Korea.

Collins, R. M. (2019). *North Korea's Organization and Guidance Department: The Control Tower of Human Rights Denial*. Washington, DC: Committee for Human Rights in North Korea.

Collins, R. M. & Oh, A. M. (2017). *From Cradle to Grave: The Path of North Korean Innocents*. Washington, DC: Committee for Human Rights in North Korea.

Cumings, B. (1997). *Korea's Place in the Sun: A Modern History*. 1st ed. New York: Norton.

Daily NK. (2017). *The Creation of the North Korean Market System*. Seoul: Green People.

Daily NK. (2018). "North Korean Markets Insulated from Sanctions, Though Not Forever." March 7. www.dailynk.com/english/north-korean-markets-insulated-fro/.

David-West, A. (2013). North Korea and the Contradiction of Inversion: Dictatorship, Markets, Social Reform. *North Korean Review* 9(1), 100–113.

Demick, B. (2009). *Nothing to Envy: Ordinary Lives in North Korea*. New York: Spiegel & Grau.

Diamond, L. J. (1994). Toward Democratic Consolidation. *Journal of Democracy* 5(3), 4–17.

Dickson, B. (2007). Integrating Wealth and Power in China: The Communist Party's Embrace of the Private Sector. *The China Quarterly* (192), 827-854.

Dickson, B. (2016). *The Dictator's Dilemma: The Chinese Communist Party's Strategy for Survival*. New York: Oxford University Press.

Dickson, B. (2020). "The U.S. Is Using Harsh Language about the Chinese Communist Party. Who Joins the CCP – and Why?" *Washington Post*, December 3. www.washingtonpost.com/politics/2020/07/24/us-is-using-harsh-language-about-chinese-communist-party-who-joins-ccp-why/.

Dimitrov, M. K. (2013). *Why Communism Did Not Collapse: Understanding Authoritarian Regime Resilience in Asia and Europe*. Cambridge: Cambridge University Press.

DPRK Today. (2020). "People Move to New Houses in North Hamgyong Province." December 9. https://dprktoday.com/abroad/news/25903?lang.

Dukalskis, A. (2016). North Korea's Shadow Economy: A Force for Authoritarian Resilience or Corrosion? *Europe-Asia Studies* 68(3), 487–507.

Dukalskis, A. (2017). *The Authoritarian Public Sphere: Legitimation and Autocratic Power in North Korea, Burma, and China*. London: Routledge.

Dukalskis, A. & Gerschewski, J. (2017). What Autocracies Say (and What Citizens Hear): Proposing Four Mechanisms of Autocratic Legitimation. *Contemporary Politics* 23(3), 251–68.

Dukalskis, A. & Joo, H. M. (2020). Everyday Authoritarianism in North Korea. *Europe-Asia Studies*. Online First. www.tandfonline.com/doi/abs/10.1080/09668136.2020.1840517.

Edwards, M. (2009). *Civil Society*. Cambridge: Cambridge University Press.

Ekiert, G., Yan, X. & Perry, E. J. (2020). *Ruling by Other Means: State-Mobilized Movements*. New York: Cambridge University Press.

Fahy, S. (2015). *Marching through Suffering: Loss and Survival in North Korea*. New York: Columbia University Press.

Fahy, S. (2019). *Dying for Rights: Putting North Korea's Human Rights Abuses on the Record*. New York: Columbia University Press.

Fifield, A. (2019). *The Great Successor: The Divinely Perfect Destiny of Brilliant Comrade Kim Jong-un*. New York: PublicAffairs.

Foley, M. & Edwards, B. (1996). The Paradox of Civil Society. *Journal of Democracy* 7(3), 38–52.

Frank, R. (2021). "Key Results of the Eighth Party Congress in North Korea." 38 North. January 15. www.38north.org/2021/01/key-results-of-the-eighth-party-congress-in-north-korea-part-1-of-2/.

Frank, R. & Park, P. H. (2012). From Monolithic Totalitarian to Collective Authoritarian Leadership? Performance-Based Legitimacy and Power Transfer in North Korea. *North Korean Review* 8(2), 32–49.

Frantz, E. (2018). *Authoritarianism: What Everyone Needs to Know*. New York: Oxford University Press.

Frantz, E., Kendall-Taylor, A., Wright, J. & Xu, X. (2020). Personalization of Power and Repression in Dictatorships. *The Journal of Politics* 82(1), 372–77.

Gallagher, M. (2004). China: The Limits of China in a Late Leninist State. In M. Alagappa, ed., *Civil Society and Political Change in Asia: Expanding and Contracting Democratic Space*. Stanford, CA: Stanford University Press, 419–52.

Gandhi, J. & Przeworski, A. (2007). Authoritarian Institutions and the Survival of Autocrats. *Comparative Political Studies* 40(11), 1279–301.

Geddes, B., Wright, J. & Frantz, E. (2018). *How Dictatorships Work: Power, Personalization, and Collapse*. Cambridge: Cambridge University Press.

Giacomo, C. (2017). "Decoding Dress in North Korea." *New York Times*, October 16. www.nytimes.com/2017/10/16/fashion/decoding-dress-in-north-korea.html.

Gray, K. and Lee, J. W. (2021). *North Korea and the Geopolitics of Development*. Cambridge: Cambridge University Press.

Greitens, S. C. (2016). *Dictators and Their Secret Police: Coercive Institutions and State Violence*. New York: Cambridge University Press.

Greitens, S. C. (2019). Explaining Economic Order in North Korea. In G. Brazinksy, ed., *Korea and the World*. Lanham, MD: Lexington Books, 129–55.

Greitens, S. C. (2020). The Saohei Campaign, Protection Umbrellas, and China's Changing Political-Legal Apparatus. *China Leadership Monitor*. September 1. www.prcleader.org/greitens-1.

Habermas, J. (1991). *The Structural Transformation of the Public Sphere: An Inquiry Into a Category of Bourgeois Society*. Cambridge, MA: MIT Press.

Haggard, S., Lee, J. & Noland, M. (2012). Integration in the Absence of Institutions: China-North Korea Cross-Border Exchange. *Journal of Asian Economics* 23(2), 130–145.

Haggard, S. & Noland, M. (2007). *Famine in North Korea: Markets, Aid, and Reform.* New York: Columbia University Press.

Haggard, S. & Noland, M. (2011). *Witness to Transformation: Refugee Insights into North Korea.* Washington, DC: Peterson Institute for International Economics.

Haggard, S. & Noland, M. (2017). *Hard Target: Sanctions, Inducements, and the Case of North Korea.* Palo Alto, CA: Stanford University Press.

Haggard, S. & Noland, M. (2018). Networks, Trust and Trade: The Microeconomics of China-North Korea Integration. *Asian Economic Journal* 32(3), 277-299.

Hassig, R. C. & Oh, K. D. (2015). *The Hidden People of North Korea: Everyday Life in the Hermit Kingdom.* Lanham, MD: Rowman & Littlefield.

Hastings, J. V. (2016). *A Most Enterprising Country: North Korea in the Global Economy.* Ithaca, NY: Cornell University Press.

Hastings, J. V., Wertz, D. & Yeo, A. (2021). *Market Activities and the Building Blocks of Civil Society in North Korea.* Washington, DC: National Committee on North Korea.

Hawk, D. (2012). *Hidden Gulag: Exposing North Korea's Vast System of Lawless Imprisonment.* 2nd ed. Washington, DC: US Committee for Human Rights in North Korea.

Howard, M. M. (2003). *The Weakness of Civil Society in Post-Communist Europe.* Cambridge: Cambridge University Press.

Huang, H. (2018). The Pathology of Hard Propaganda. *The Journal of Politics* 80, 1034–38.

Hur, A. (2020). Refugee Perceptions toward Democratic Citizenship: A Narrative Analysis of North Koreans. *Comparative Politics* 52, 473–93.

Institute for Peace and Unification Studies (IPUS). (2020). *Bukhan joomin tongil uisik, 2019.* [North Koreans' thoughts on unification, 2019]. Seoul, South Korea: Institute for Peace and Unification Studies.

Jackman, R. W. and Miller, R. A. (1998). Social Capital and Politics. *Annual Review of Political Science* 1(1), 47–73.

Jeong, A. & Martin, T. (2019). "Kim Jong-un Purges Wealthy Elite and Opponents of Outreach to U.S." *Wall Street Journal*, February 19. www.wsj.com/articles/kim-jong-un-purges-north-korean-elite-in-violent-crackdown-11550593810.

Jong, S. Y. (2020). "Minister of State Construction Control Censured by Government." Daily NK. August 19. www.dailynk.com/english/minister-state-construction-control-censured-government.

Joo, H. M. (2010). Visualizing the Invisible Hands: The Shadow Economy in North Korea. *Economy and Society* 39(1), 110–45.

Joo, H. M. (2014). Hidden Transcripts in Marketplaces: Politicized Discourses in the North Korean Shadow Economy. *The Pacific Review* 27(1), 49–71.

Kang, D. C. (2012). They Think They're Normal: Enduring Questions and New Research on North Korea: A Review Essay. *International Security* 36(3), 142–71.

Kang, M. J. (2018). "Some Neighborhood Watch Leaders Picked by More Democratic Process." *DailyNK*. March 26. www.dailynk.com/english/some-neighborhood-watch-leaders-pi/.

Kendall-Taylor, A., Frantz, F. & Wright, J. (2017). The Global Rise of Personalized Politics: It's Not Just Dictators Anymore. *The Washington Quarterly* 40(1), 7–19.

Kern H. L. & Hainmueller, J. (2017). Opium for the Masses: How Foreign Media Can Stabilize Authoritarian Regimes. *Political Analysis* 17, 377–99.

Kim, B. Y. (2017). *Unveiling the North Korean Economy: Collapse and Transition*. Cambridge: Cambridge University Press.

Kim, B. Y. (2019). "Kim in a Cage." *Joongang Ilbo*, December 18. https://koreajoongangdaily.joins.com/2019/12/18/columns/Kim-in-a%20cage/3071650.html?detailWord.

Kim, B. Y. & Kim, S. H. (2019). Market Activities and Trust of North Korean Refugees. *Asian Economic Policy Review* 14(2), 238–57.

Kim, S. (2013). *Everyday Life in the North Korean Revolution, 1945–1950*. Ithaca, NY: Cornell University Press.

Kim, S. H. (2000). *The Politics of Democratization in Korea: The Role of Civil Society*. Pittsburgh, PA: University of Pittsburgh Press.

Kim, S. J. & Yang, M. S. (2015). *The Growth of the Informal Economy in North Korea*. Seoul: Korean Institute for National Unification.

Kim, S. K., Lee, K. C., Do, K. O. & Hong, J. H. (2019). *White Paper on Human Rights in North Korea, 2019*. Seoul: KINU.

Kim, Y. (2019). *North Korea's Mobile Telecommunications and Private Transportation Services in the Kim Jong-Un Era*. Washington, DC: Committee for Human Rights in North Korea.

Kim, Y. (2020). *North Korean Phone Money: Airtime Transfers as a Precursor to Mobile Payment System*. Special Report, no. 481. United States Institute for Peace: Washington, DC.

Kim, Y. H. (2014). *Jipkwon 2 nyeon-cha, Kim Jong-un jeonggwonui gyeongje-gaehyeok pyeongga* [Evaluating Kim Jong-un's economic reform in his second year of rule]. *KDI North Korea Economic Review* (3), 25–38.

Koen, V. & Beom, J. (2020). *"North Korea: the Last Transition Economy? OECD Economics Department Working Papers,"* no. 1607. Paris, France: OECD.

Korea Central News Agency (KCNA). (2016). "Full Text of Supreme Leader Kim Jong-un's Report to the Seventh Congress of the Workers' Party of Korea on the Work of the Central Committee." KCNA Watch. June 16. https://kcnawatch.org/newstream/1546587552-192142420/supreme-leader-kim-jong-uns-report-to-the-seventh-congress-of-the-workers-party-of-korea-on-the-work-of-the-central-committee-full-text/?t=1600747374958.

Korea Peace Now. (2019). *Human Costs and Gendered Impact of Sanctions on North Korea*. Korea Peace Now.

Kretchun, N. & Kim, J. (2012). *A Quiet Opening: North Koreans in a Changing Media Environment*. Washington, DC: InterMedia, 2012.

Kretchun, N., Lee, C. & Tuohy, S. (2017). *Compromising Connectivity: Information Dynamics between the State and Society in a Digitizing North Korea*. Washington, DC: InterMedia.

Kuran, T. (1991). Now Out of Never: The Element of Surprise in the East European Revolution of 1989. *World Politics* 44(1), 7–48.

Lankov, A. (2006). Bitter Taste of Paradise: North Korean Refugees in South Korea. *Journal of East Asian Studies* 6, 105–37.

Lankov, A. (2013a). *The Real North Korea: Life and Politics in the Failed Stalinist Utopia*. New York: Oxford University Press.

Lankov, A. (2013b). "Nouveau Riche in Pyongyang," *Korea Times*, June 16. www.koreatimes.co.kr/www/news/opinon/2013/06/304_137572.html.

Lankov, A., Kwak, I. O. & Cho, C. B. (2012). The Organizational Life: Daily Surveillance and Daily Resistance in North Korea. *Journal of East Asian Studies* 12(2), 193–214.

Lankov, A., Ward, P., Yoo, H. W. & Kim. J. Y. (2017). Making Money in the State: North Korea's Pseudo-State Enterprises in the Early 2000s. *Journal of East Asian Studies* 17(1), 51–67.

Lee, J. H. (2019a). "North Korea's 'Marketized Economy' Already at an Irreversible Stage." *Hankyoreh*. February 5. http://english.hani.co.kr/arti/english_edition/e_northkorea/881048.html.

Lee, J. H. (2019b). "The 'Masters of Money' behind North Korea's Development Projects." *Hankyoreh*. February 6. http://english.hani.co.kr/arti/english_edition/e_northkorea/881066.html.

Lee, J. (2018). *Choegeun bukhan uui kyungjae jeongchaek pyungga mit hyanghoo jeonmang* [Outlook and direction of North Korea's recent economic policy]. Sejong City, South Korea: Korea Development Institute.

Lee, S. S. (2012). Paradox of Neoliberalism: Arab Spring's Implications on North Korea. *North Korean Review* 8(1), 53–66.

Linz, J. J. & Stepan, A. (1996). *Problems of Democratic Transition and Consolidation: Southern Europe, South America, and Post-Communist Europe*. Baltimore: Johns Hopkins University Press.

Mansourov, A. (2013). "North Korea: What Jang's Execution Means for the Future." 38 North. December 13. www.38north.org/2013/12/aman sourov121313/.

McEachern, P. (2010). *Inside the Red Box: North Korea's Post-totalitarian Politics*. New York: Columbia University Press.

National Committee on North Korea (NCNK). (2019). "Kim Jong-un's 2019 New Year Address." Translated from *Rodong Sinmun*. www.ncnk.org /resources/publications/kimjongun_2019_newyearaddress.pdf/file_view.

National Committee on North Korea (NCNK). (2020). *Report of the Fifth Plenary Meeting of the 7th Central Committee of the WPK: Kim Jong-un's 2020 New Year Address*. January 1. www.ncnk.org/resources/publications/ kju_2020_new_years_plenum_report.pdf/file_view.

O'Carroll, C. & Brehm, R. (2018). "North Korea in October 2018: A Month in Review." NK Pro. Korea Risk. October 25. www.nknews.org/pro/north-korea-a-month-in-review-3/.

Park, S. (2018). "A Changing North Korea." Liberty in North Korea. www .libertyinnorthkorea.org/learn-a-changing-north-korea/.

Park, S. H. (2019). The New Policy Frame in Recent Economic and Social Changes in North Korea. *Korea Observer* 50(4), 483–503.

Park, Y. J, Cho, J. A., Hong, J. H., Joung, E. H., Jeong, E. M., Lee, S., Jeon, Y. & Kang, H. J. (2018). *Kim Jong-un sidae bukhan kyungjae sahoe 8-dae byunhwa* [Eight Changes in North Korean Economy and Society under the Kim Jong-un Regime]. Seoul: Korean Institute for National Unification.

Person, J. (n.d.). *The 1967 Purge of the Gapsan Faction and Establishment of the Monolithic Ideological System*. North Korea International Document Project e-Dossier no. 15. www.wilsoncenter.org/publication-series/nkidp-e-dossier-series.

Putnam, R. D. (1993). *Making Democracy Work: Civic Traditions in Modern Italy*. Princeton, NJ: Princeton University Press.

Putnam, R. D. (2000). *Bowling Alone: The Collapse and Revival of American Community*. New York: Simon & Schuster.

Ri, H. N. (2019). "Capitalist Society Has No Future." *Rodong Sinmun*, January 10. https://rodong.rep.kp/en/index.php?strPageID=SF01_02_01&newsID=2019-01-10-0004.

RFA. (2018). *"Buk gongsik sijang ggojonhi jeungga* [North Korea's official markets consistently increasing, numbering over 480]. Radio Free Asia. February 3. www.rfa.org/korean/in_focus/ne-jn-02022018151709.html.

Robinson, W. C. (2019). *Lost Generation: The Health and Human Rights of North Korean Children, 1990–2018.* Washington, DC: Committee for Human Rights in North Korea.

Rodong Sinmun. (2013). "Legitimacy of Our Party's Ideology of Building a Socialist Civilization." *Rodong Sinmun,* July 14.

Rodong Sinmun. (2019). "Let Us Step Up Construction of Highly Civilized Socialist Country."*Rodong Sinmun,* January 18. https://rodong.rep.kp/en/index.php?strPageID=SF01_02_01&newsID=2019-01-28-0001.

Rodong Sinmun. (2020a). *Deowook wonbyuk hagae* [Towards perfection]. *Rodong Sinmun,* July 13. https://rodong.rep.kp/ko/index.php?strPageID=SF01_02_01&newsID=2020-07-13-0002.

Rodong Sinmun. (2020b). "Fundamentals of Invincibility of Our-Style Socialism." *Rodong Sinmun,* May 30. https://rodong.rep.kp/en/index.php?strPageID=SF01_02_01&newsID=2020-05-30-0003.

Ryall, J. (2019). "Pyongyang Calling: How North Korea Pressures Defectors to the South." *South China Morning Post,* July 13. www.scmp.com/news/asia/east-asia/article/3018449/pyongyang-calling-how-north-korea-pressures-defectors-south.

Saucedo, N. (2020). "Using Fashion as Silent Protest in North Korea." Human Rights Foundation. March 12. https://hrf.org/press_posts/how-north-koreans-dissent-through-fashion/.

Schwartz, F. (2003). What Is Civil Society? In F. J. Schwartz and S. J. Pharr, eds., *The State of Civil Society in Japan.* Cambridge: Cambridge University Press, 23–41.

Scott, J. C. (1990). *Arts of Resistance: The Hidden Transcript of Subordinate Groups.* New Haven: Yale University Press.

Seth, M. J. (2016). *A Concise History of Modern Korea: From the Late Nineteenth Century to the Present.* Lanham, MD: Rowman & Littlefield.

Shin, G. W. (2006). *Ethnic Nationalism in Korea: Genealogy, Politics, and Legacy.* Stanford, CA: Stanford University Press.

Shirk, S. L. (2007). *China: Fragile Superpower.* New York: Oxford University Press.

Silberstein, B. K. (2020a). "The North Korean Economy: The Pandemic and North Korean Food Security." 38 North. May 28. www.38north.org/2020/05/bkatzeffsilberstein052820/.

Silberstein, B. K (2020b). "The North Korean Economy: Assessing the Flood Damage. 38 North. October 16. www.38north.org/2020/10/bkatzeffsilber stein101620/.

Smith, H. (2015). *North Korea: Markets and Military Rule*. Cambridge: Cambridge University Press.

Song, J., & Denney, S. (2019). Studying North Korea through North Korean Migrants: Lessons from the Field. *Critical Asian Studies* 51(3), 451–66.

Song, W., and Wright, J. (2018). The North Korean Autocracy in Comparative Perspective. *Journal of East Asian Studies* 18(2), 157–80.

Stewart, E. (2018). "Watch the 'Movie Trailer' Trump Showed Kim Jong-un about North Korea's Possible Future." Vox Media. www.vox.com/world/ 2018/6/12/17452876/trump-kim-jong-un-meeting-north-korea-video.

Svolik, M. W. (2012). *The Politics of Authoritarian Rule*. New York: Cambridge University Press.

Taylor, C. (1990). Modes of Civil Society. *Public Culture* 3(1), 95–118.

Teets, J. C. (2013). Let Many Civil Societies Bloom: The Rise of Consultative Authoritarianism in China. *The China Quarterly* 213, 19–38.

Teets, J. C. (2014). *Civil Society under Authoritarianism: The China Model*. New York: Cambridge University Press.

Tismaneanu, V. (2013). Ideological Erosion and the Breakdown of Communist Regimes. In M. K. Dimitrov, ed., *Why Communism Did Not Collapse: Understanding Authoritarian Regime Resilience in Asia and Europe*. Cambridge: Cambridge University Press, 67–98.

Tsai K. S. (2007). *Capitalism without Democracy: The Private Sector in Contemporary China*. Ithaca, NY: Cornell University Press.

Tudor, D. & Pearson, J. (2015). *North Korea Confidential: Private Markets, Fashion Trends, Prison Camps, Dissenters and Defectors*. North Clarendon, VT: Tuttle.

United Nations Commission of Inquiry (UNCOI). (2014). *Report of the Commission of Inquiry on Human Rights in the Democratic People's Republic of Korea*. Geneva, Switzerland: UNHRC.

United Nations, DPRK Resident Coordinator. (2019). *DPR Korea Needs and Priorities*. March 9. https://dprkorea.un.org/en/10164-dpr-korea-needs-and-priorities-2019.

United Nations Security Council (UNSC). (2020). *Report of the Panel of Experts Established Pursuant to Resolution 1874*. S/2020/151. March 2.

von Haldenwang, C. (2017). The Relevance of Legitimation – A New Framework for Analysis. *Contemporary Politics* 23(3), 269–86.

Ward, P. (2020). "North Korea is on a Crusade against Drugs, Crime and 'Capitalist Culture.'" NK News. December 2. www.nknews.org/pro/north-korea-is-on-a-crusade-against-drugs-crime-and-capitalist-culture/?t=1607218550293.

Wedeen, L. (2015). *Ambiguities of Domination: Politics, Rhetoric, and Symbols in Contemporary Syria*. 2nd edn. Chicago: University of Chicago Press.

Wertz, D. (2020). "Can Kim Jong-un Use the Pandemic to Restore State Control Over the Economy?" 38 North. May 15. www.38north.org/2020/05/dwertz051520/.

Williams, M. (2019). *Digital Trenches: North Korea's Information Counter-Offensive*. Washington, DC: Committee for Human Rights in North Korea.

Wong, S. & Pearson, J. (2017). "Colas, Cigarettes: North Korea Airline Diversifies as Threats Mount of Sanctions." Reuters. April 21. www.reuters.com/article/us-northkorea-usa-airkoryo/colas-cigarettes-north-korea-airline-diversifies-as-threats-mount-of-sanctions-idUSKBN17N020.

Yang, M. S. (2020). *An Assessment of Economic Issues Raised in the 7th WPK Central Committee's 5th Plenary Session: Reorganizing the Economic Management System's Foundation Amid Emphasis on 'Self-Reliance.'* Institute for Far Eastern Studies, no. 90. Seoul, South Korea: IFES. http://ifes.kyungnam.ac.kr/eng/FRM/FRM_0401V.aspx?code=FRM200108_0001.

Yeo, A. (2017). Evaluating the Scope of People-to-People Engagement in North Korea, 1995–2012. *Asian Perspective* 41(2), 309–39.

Yeo, A. (2020). Assessing Domestic Change and Continuity in North Korea. *Asian Studies Review* 44(4), 1–11.

Yeo, A. & Chubb, D. L. (2018). *North Korean Human Rights: Activists and Networks*. New York: Cambridge University Press.

Yonhap News. (2017). "N. Korea Emphasizes Corporate Profits in Economic Policies." December 4. https://en.yna.co.kr/view/AEN20170404013600315.

Yonhap News. (2020). "N. Korea's Trade with China down 67 pct Amid Pandemic." August 20. https://en.yna.co.kr/view/AEN20200820001200320.

Young, B. (2020). "Why Kim Yo-Jong Would Take Over North Korea If Kim Jong-un Died." *The National Interest*. May 5. https://nationalinterest.org/blog/korea-watch/why-kim-yo-jong-would-take-over-north-korea-if-kim-jong-un-died-151071

Acknowledgments and Afterword

As with other Korean-Americans interested in Korea-related affairs, I have followed North Korean politics since my time as an undergraduate student in the late 1990s. This Element offers two decades of my own thinking and research on North Korea and the prospects for domestic change. I am grateful to the series editors, Erin Chung, Ben Read, and especially Mary Alice Haddad for providing guidance and allowing me to publish *State, Society, and Markets in North Korea* in their new Cambridge Elements series on Politics and Society in East Asia. I also thank James Baker and Priyanka Durai for their support during the production process. Helpful suggestions from an anonymous reviewer and an able copyeditor (Alexander Macleod) improved this manuscript as well.

My research greatly benefited from a five-year collaborative project, "Exploring the Black Box of North Korea in a Globalized Context," under the auspices of the Center for Strategic and International Studies (CSIS) Korea Chair, made possible with a Laboratory Program for Korean Studies grant through the Ministry of Education of the Republic of Korea and the Korean Studies Promotion Service of the Academy of Korean Studies (AKS-2016-LAB-2250001). I thank AKS for their generous funding, and the CSIS Korea Chair and several current and former staff members including Victor Cha (senior adviser and project director), Marie Dumond, Lisa Collins, Sang-Jun Lee, Andy Lim, and Seiyeon Ji for their assistance. This Element is the outcome of the CSIS-AKS sponsored research. I owe a special thanks to my CSIS-AKS "lab mates" Sheena Greitens, John Delury, and Victor Cha (again) who read and commented on portions of the manuscript during our "scrub sessions."

This project also benefited from my collaboration with Justin Hastings and Daniel Wertz on a policy report on private markets and civil society building blocks in North Korea released by the National Committee on North Korea (NCNK). I wish to express my thanks to Justin and Dan for their input. I am also grateful to Sandra Fahy, who on very short notice read the entire manuscript, offering her expert suggestions. Ed Tadem and Michelle Palumbarit offered useful feedback as well when I presented my research at the University of the Philippines Center for Integrative and Development Studies. Some of the ideas in this book were reflected in a review essay I wrote for *Asian Studies Review* (*ASR*), "Assessing Domestic Change and Continuity in North Korea," and I thank *ASR* editors David Hundt and Jay Song for their input. Finally, this book would not have been completed without the excellent research assistance of Sujin Heo. Thank you Sujin for your timely assistance and for being a trustworthy sounding board.

My association with various "networks" of North Korea watchers, not all of whom agree with one another on matters of policy and principle, has proven to be invaluable. I have chosen not to name individuals here due to sensitivities with ongoing work related to North Korea, but you know who you are, and I thank you for sharing your thoughts on North Korea, whether it pertains to humanitarian engagement, human rights, and/or security and foreign policy. One organization I will acknowledge is NCNK. NCNK has remained true to its mission of fostering mutual understanding and trust between the United States and North Korea while remaining open to a variety of viewpoints on how best to promote engagement, cooperation, tension reduction, and peace. I have learned much through friendships and connections with other members, and have been humbled on several occasions by their extraordinary work to engage the North Korean people while also not shying away from addressing difficult policy questions. The views here of course are my own, and not those of NCNK or any of its members.

The book itself was written during the course of the pandemic in 2020–21, during which my wife, two kids, and I were confined to our condo in Manila for over one year. As challenging as writing may have been, I am grateful to have spent that time together. I thank my wife, Yoon, for creating moments for me to work despite her own demanding schedule. To Joshua and Joyce, my apologies for often ignoring your pleas to play, but I know you understand.

I can only begin to fathom the effects of COVID-19 in a country like North Korea. Although the number of deaths directly attributable to COVID-19 may be relatively few (North Korea has reported zero cases of COVID-19 for over one year), its impact on the economy surpasses that of sanctions. As with most disasters, whether natural or human made, it is the ordinary and vulnerable who suffer the most. Markets can help alleviate some of that suffering. So might the presence of even a limited civil society that works in conjunction with the state. Regardless of whether markets can help foster the emergence of a limited civil society, state-society relations in North Korea will certainly undergo further transformation after the pandemic. I dedicate this book to the North Korean people.

Manila, Philippines
April 2021
Andrew Yeo

Cambridge Elements ⁼

Politics and Society in East Asia

Erin Aeran Chung
Johns Hopkins University

Erin Aeran Chung is the Charles D. Miller Associate Professor of East Asian Politics in the Department of Political Science at the Johns Hopkins University. She specializes in East Asian political economy, international migration, and comparative racial politics. She is the author of *Immigration and Citizenship in Japan* (Cambridge, 2010, 2014; Japanese translation, Akashi Shoten, 2012) and *Immigrant Incorporation in East Asian Democracies* (Cambridge, 2020). Her research has been supported by grants from the Academy of Korean Studies, the Japan Foundation, the Japan Foundation Center for Global Partnership, the Social Science Research Council, and the American Council of Learned Societies.

Mary Alice Haddad
Wesleyan University

Mary Alice Haddad is the John E. Andrus Professor of Government, East Asian Studies, and Environmental Studies at Wesleyan University. Her research focuses on democracy, civil society, and environmental politics in East Asia as well as city diplomacy around the globe. A Fulbright and Harvard Academy scholar, Haddad is author of *Effective Advocacy: Lessons from East Asia's Environmentalists* (MIT, 2021), *Building Democracy in Japan* (Cambridge, 2012), and *Politics and Volunteering in Japan* (Cambridge, 2007), and co-editor of *Greening East Asia* (University of Washington, 2021), and *NIMBY is Beautiful* (Berghahn Books, 2015). She has published in journals such as Comparative Political Studies, Democratization, Journal of Asian Studies, and Nonprofit and Voluntary Sector Quarterly, with writing for the public appearing in the Asahi Shimbun, the Hartford Courant, and the South China Morning Post.

Benjamin L. Read
University of California, Santa Cruz

Benjamin L. Read is a professor of Politics at the University of California, Santa Cruz. His research has focused on local politics in China and Taiwan, and he also writes about issues and techniques in field research. He is author of *Roots of the State: Neighborhood Organization and Social Networks in Beijing and Taipei* (Stanford, 2012), coauthor of *Field Research in Political Science: Practices and Principles* (Cambridge, 2015), and co-editor of *Local Organizations and Urban Governance in East and Southeast Asia: Straddling State and Society* (Routledge, 2009). His work has appeared in journals such as Comparative Political Studies, Comparative Politics, the Journal of Conflict Resolution, the China Journal, the China Quarterly, and the Washington Quarterly, as well as several edited books.

About the Series

The Cambridge Elements series on Politics and Society in East Asia offers original, multidisciplinary contributions on enduring and emerging issues in the dynamic region of East Asia by leading scholars in the field. Suitable for general readers and specialists alike, these short, peer-reviewed volumes examine common challenges and patterns within the region while identifying key differences between countries. The series consists of two types of contributions: 1) authoritative field surveys of established concepts and themes that offer roadmaps for further research; and 2) new research on emerging issues that challenge conventional understandings of East Asian politics and society. Whether focusing on an individual country or spanning the region, the contributions in this series connect regional trends with points of theoretical debate in the social sciences and will stimulate productive interchanges among students, researchers, and practitioners alike.

Printed in the United States
by Baker & Taylor Publisher Services